Recla
after Trauma

"A brilliantly presented book on the most debilitating health issues of the twenty-first century: trauma and PTSD. *Reclaiming Life after Trauma* is a road map to rewiring the brain and embodying wellness. A well-timed book, I can confidently affirm that it will have a remarkable positive impact on people's lives."

HAKIMA AMRI, PH.D., PROFESSOR OF BIOCHEMISTRY AND PHYSIOLOGY
AND DIRECTOR OF THE INTEGRATIVE MEDICINE GRADUATE PROGRAM AT
GEORGETOWN UNIVERSITY AND AUTHOR OF *AVICENNA'S MEDICINE*

"To recover from trauma is to awaken the seed of resilience inherent within each of us and to stabilize our renewed inner experience with supportive habits into a new way of being. The practice of yoga and meditation with cognitive-behavioral therapy forms an effective partnership to engage the physiological and structural aspects of the body and identify thought patterns that keep us in the past. *Reclaiming Life after Trauma* skillfully shows us that no matter what the source of the trauma, post-traumatic growth and full recovery are within reach."

SHANTI SHANTI KAUR KHALSA, PH.D., DIRECTOR OF INTERNATIONAL
KUNDALINI YOGA THERAPY PROFESSIONAL TRAINING

"Integrating cognitive behavioral therapy with Kundalini Yoga, Mintie and Staples weave the wisdom of both disciplines to effectively reduce suffering present with trauma. Practical strategies engage the reader to increase his or her awareness of maladaptive thinking patterns and create impact on his or her own pain patterns. Breathwork and go-to steps encourage participation. Case studies illustrate the process of change, including stumbling blocks met along the way. Well referenced yet easily understood. This is important information to be shared with professionals and the general public alike."

JUDITH PENTZ, M.D., INTEGRATIVE PSYCHIATRIST AND
ASSISTANT PROFESSOR IN THE DEPARTMENT OF PSYCHIATRY
AND BEHAVIORAL SCIENCES AT THE UNIVERSITY OF NEW MEXICO

"In this wise and compassionate book, the authors offer a clear, practical, step-by-step guide for those with PTSD who wish to find a path to joy, hope, and freedom from suffering. Grounded in research based on their wealth of professional experience and integrating key tenets, strategies, and principles from both cognitive-behavioral therapy and Kundalini Yoga, their innovative program includes a range of simple but powerful tools, which can be used either at home or in a therapeutic setting. Although specifically designed for those who have experienced trauma, this program would be beneficial to anyone seeking to lead a more joyful, peaceful, and fulfilling life. The book is a wonderful read, eloquently written and deftly interwoven with compelling stories of men and women who have used the tools of this program to transform their lives."

KIM INNES, M.S.P.H., PH.D, ASSOCIATE PROFESSOR
AT WEST VIRGINIA UNIVERSITY SCHOOL OF PUBLIC HEALTH

Reclaiming Life after Trauma

Healing PTSD with Cognitive-Behavioral Therapy and Yoga

Daniel Mintie, LCSW,
and
Julie K. Staples, Ph.D.

Healing Arts Press
Rochester, Vermont

Healing Arts Press
One Park Street
Rochester, Vermont 05767
www.HealingArtsPress.com

Text stock is SFI certified

Healing Arts Press is a division of Inner Traditions International

Note to the reader: *This book is intended as an informational guide. The remedies, approaches, and techniques described herein are meant to supplement, and not to be a substitute for, professional medical care or treatment. They should not be used to treat a serious ailment without prior consultation with a qualified health care professional.*

A CIP record for this title is available from the Library of Congress

ISBN 978-1-62055-634-4 (print)
ISBN 978-1-62055-635-1 (e-book)

Printed and bound in the United States by Lake Book Manufacturing, Inc.
The text stock is SFI certified. The Sustainable Forestry Initiative® program promotes sustainable forest management.

10 9 8 7 6 5 4 3 2 1

Text design and layout by Priscilla Baker
This book was typeset in Garamond Premier Pro with Utopia Std, Gill Sans MT Pro and ITC Avant Garde Gothic Std used as display typefaces
Yoga illustrations by Dana Verkouteren

To send correspondence to the authors of this book, mail a first-class letter to the authors c/o Inner Traditions • Bear & Company, One Park Street, Rochester, VT 05767, and we will forward the communication. You may contact either author directly at **www.integrative-trauma-recovery.com**.

This book is dedicated to the men, women, and children of North and South America, Europe, Asia, and the Middle East we've had the honor of working with over many years. Their courage, openheartedness, and determination to heal from the aftereffects of war, natural disaster, and personal tragedy have shown us anew what it means to be human, to be resilient, to reclaim life after trauma.

Please know that individuals' names and any details that might personally identify them have been changed.

Contents

Acknowledgments

We are grateful to many people whose lives and work have made this book possible. Foremost among them are our teachers and mentors Robert Aitken, Willigis Jäger, Yogi Bhajan, Ph.D., and David Burns, M.D.

Numerous colleagues have made invaluable contributions to this book and to the Integrative Trauma Recovery Program (ITRP) upon which the book is based. Shanti Shanti Kaur Khalsa, Ph.D., developed the yoga portion of the ITRP based on Kundalini Yoga as taught by Yogi Bhajan® and provided generous consultation on its delivery. Siri Neel Kaur Khalsa kindly reviewed the yoga sections of the manuscript for accuracy. Sat Bir Singh Khalsa, Ph.D., collaborated on our research study of the ITRP and gave us expert advice on the study design. Mary Bibb, M.D., provided astute feedback on the cognitive-behavioral therapy (CBT) portions of the manuscript, and Matthew May, M.D., made essential contributions to the CBT the book presents.

Introduction

Trauma, which is the Greek word for "wound," is the most widespread form of suffering in the world today. No one escapes it. Large or small, physical or psychological, injury is simply one price we pay for a life on earth. Buddhism's first noble truth tells us "Life is suffering." On this point all great world religions agree. The day of our birth is difficult. So too is the day of our death. And troubles arise every day in between.

Many people who experience trauma—physical or sexual assault, loss of a loved one, illness, automobile accident, forced migration, military firefights—have what we can call *healthy* negative emotion and move on with their lives. Healthy negative emotion might be sadness at the death of a friend or anger at being attacked. We don't need psychotherapy for healthy negative emotion. It would seem wrong not to feel sadness at the death of a loved one. Such sadness is part and parcel of our humanity and love, a testament to what we shared with another human being. And feeling no flash of anger when we are attacked might signal a deeper problem, perhaps with self-esteem. We are hardwired for such emotions the same way we are hardwired, when injured, to feel physical pain. These healthy negative emotions help us live and die well, adding meaning and texture to our lives.

Something different happens for millions of other trauma survivors. For them a secondary form of suffering is added to the pain of the injury itself. We call this secondary suffering post-traumatic stress disorder (PTSD), a state of ongoing uneasiness expressed in our bodies, emotions, sense of worth, sleep patterns, and relationships with others. *Unhealthy* negative emotions—bitterness, rage, despair, feelings of worthlessness—characterize PTSD. And while an initial trauma may last but a few seconds, these unhealthy negative emotions can continue for years. Left untreated, they may follow us to the grave.

If you are experiencing this kind of post-traumatic suffering, this book was written for you. It is based on the authors' decades of experience helping people of all ages heal from PTSD. This book is our way of walking with you the road to wellness. Your path will be somewhat different from anyone else's path. We've learned we cannot "treat PTSD" the way a doctor might treat a bacterial infection. Unlike a bacterium, there is nothing called "PTSD" in nature. PTSD is a cognitive construct, useful for diagnosis and research, that changes over time as our thinking about trauma evolves. So while we cannot "treat PTSD," the good news is we don't have to—because nobody "has" it. What millions of traumatized people *do* have—currently about 7 percent of the United States population—are unhelpful beliefs about themselves, negative thought patterns, unhealthy negative emotions, sleep problems, and difficulty relating to others. Any and all of these we can and regularly *do* treat with the drug-free, cutting-edge integrative approaches you'll learn in this book.

Here's more good news: You can successfully treat *yourself.* This book will give you the tools to do so. Because trauma affects both body and mind you'll learn powerful, evidence-based approaches to healing both the physical and the psychological manifestations of PTSD. You can learn these tools in the privacy of your home and immediately put them to use. If you do so there's a very high probability that, like many thousands of others who've walked this path, you too will reclaim a life of physical and emotional wellness, a life marked by peace, joy, sound sleep, and an abiding sense of self-worth. It is our deep hope that you will do exactly this. And it is our deep honor and joy to walk this way with you.

1

Roots of the Problem

Trauma itself does not create the set of cognitive, emotional, behavioral, and physical changes we group together and call PTSD. This form of suffering arises as the result of two changes that take place following some traumatic event or events. One change is physical, the other psychological.

Threats to our well-being trigger the body's "fight-or-flight" response, an intense activation of the *sympathetic* nervous system that prepares us to respond to emergencies. This healthy response, one that is essential to our survival, produces multiple changes in our brains and bodies. It releases stress chemicals into the bloodstream and changes blood pressure, breathing, and heart rate. If you've ever been startled by the appearance of a nearby snake you know firsthand how quickly and drastically we can shift from one internal state to another. Normally, once danger is past, the nervous system resets to *parasympathetic* functioning. Parasympathetic activity, sometimes called "rest-and-digest," is the opposite of fight-or-flight. The parasympathetic response returns the nervous system to baseline, allowing us to relax and resume our usual lives.

Trauma can interfere with this reset to baseline. PTSD might be viewed as a disorder in which the nervous system gets *stuck* in fight-or-flight. Days, weeks, or even years after the trauma we remain stressed and hypervigilant. We are unable to relax, to sleep well, or to experience positive emotion. In addition we think less clearly; fight-or-flight turns *down* the brain's cerebral cortex, that part of the frontal lobe involved in reasoning and abstract thought. We walk through our days like characters in a horror film—tense, vigilant, consciously and subconsciously scanning the shadows for what we fear could emerge from them at any time.

The second change that produces PTSD is psychological. Unhelpful beliefs such as *The world is essentially a dangerous place* or *I cannot trust others* displace earlier, helpful beliefs about ourselves, others, and the world. When triggered by events around us these unhelpful beliefs give rise to negative thoughts that produce the negative emotions that characterize PTSD. These negative emotions in turn drive self-sabotaging behaviors that actually end up confirming the new beliefs, turning them into self-fulfilling prophecies. Let's look at how this sequence of events played out for one of our patients.

Mary, a successful wilderness guide, was sexually assaulted by a client during an expedition. She subsequently decided to leave this line of work and return to school to learn computer programming. Her classmates were predominantly men and Mary found herself having panic attacks when driving into the school parking lot. She'd sit in her car until the last moment, feverishly debating whether to go to class or turn around and return home. What is going on here?

In working with Mary we discovered that after the assault her beliefs about men dramatically changed. She'd had a loving father who had died the year before she was attacked. Throughout life she'd had male friends, and as a wilderness guide, she enjoyed relating to her mostly male colleagues. After the assault Mary began believing that many, perhaps most, men might be like her attacker—dangerous predators who, given the chance, would attack her at any time. This new belief was triggered when Mary was around men, particularly in confined spaces such as the basement computer lab at school. She would then have thoughts like *He's looking at my car keys to see what I'm driving. He plans to follow me home to find out where I live.* These thoughts produced feelings of panic, entrapment, and rage. Mary's heart would begin racing and she would start to hyperventilate, dissociate from the classroom environment, and break into a cold sweat.

We can see how Mary's new belief about men, when triggered by an environmental cue, gave rise to negative thoughts that in turn produced the strong negative emotions and physiological responses typical of PTSD. What happened next is equally important. At the end of class, Mary would frequently gather up her belongings and leave before anyone else. Her fear would drive what we call *avoidance behavior* or a *security operation*. She was never actually followed home or attacked on her way home, so Mary's brain came to associate this security operation with safety. Mary came to believe that avoidance was *causing* her safety. Avoidance also kept her from getting to know individual men as human beings, allowing them to remain anonymous screens upon which Mary could project her fears. The interactions she did have with men were awkward and abrupt, which Mary saw as further proof of men's essential untrustworthiness.

Mary's experience provides a template for the human anguish we call PTSD. Let's review the main elements:

1. A traumatic event triggers changes in the body, brain, and belief system.
2. When triggered by outside events, the new unhelpful belief produces unhealthy negative thinking.
3. Unhealthy thinking produces unhealthy negative emotion, triggering the sympathetic nervous system and its fight-or-flight response.
4. Unhealthy negative emotion and physical distress drive self-sabotaging avoidance behavior.
5. Avoidance confirms the unhelpful belief.

Mary's experience also demonstrates the connection between our thought patterns and our physical experiences. While language distinguishes mental thinking from the body's physiology, these "two" are, in fact, not separate. We think with our whole body and experience physical sensation with our whole mind. If you'd like an experience of this connection right now, close your eyes and notice what happens in your body when you tell yourself *I'm so relieved!* Now again close your eyes and notice what happens in your body when you tell yourself *This is going to hurt!* Many of us will "think" the first thought by relaxing our bodies and releasing our breath. We'll "think" the second thought by contracting our bodies and holding our breath.

The book you're now reading will provide tools to address both the psychological and physical aspects of post-traumatic suffering. It's not enough to change unhealthy negative thinking if we're still walking around breathing shallowly, sweating profusely, and holding tremendous physical tension. It's also not enough to attempt to physically relax while constantly telling ourselves horrific things. We walk the road to wellness with two feet—the mental and the physical sides of human existence.

HELPFUL AND UNHELPFUL BELIEFS

"Man is what he believes," Russian playwright Anton Chekhov wrote. Modern cognitive science would agree. For better or for worse, belief lays the foundations for our lives. From earliest childhood we start believing things about ourselves, other people, and the world. Some beliefs we are taught: The earth is a sphere. The sun is at the center of our solar system. Others we teach ourselves: I am a strong, capable person. I can learn anything I want. These *helpful* beliefs support our living happy, productive lives. Most of us completely believe in gravity, something we've never seen or heard and would have a difficult time explaining to anyone else. Because we believe in it we set a cup down and don't bother to hold it in place to keep it from floating into the ethers. Think how exhausting life would be if we didn't hold this belief! Helpful beliefs, like our physical bodies themselves, provide the platform for happiness and success.

Unhelpful beliefs interfere with attaining our goals and living the lives we want. Many of us believe we're not good enough—not quite virtuous enough, or smart enough, or successful enough. Such a belief can thwart us in many ways. Let's say we're lonely and want more friends. A potential friend approaches and this triggers the belief *I'm not good enough*. We then have negative thoughts such as *If this person gets to know me, she'll reject me. It would be safer to keep my distance.* Feelings of anxiety and sadness, perhaps resentment about being in this situation, then arise. As happened in Mary's case, these feelings might well drive avoidant behavior. We shut down, turn away, and continue being alone—thus confirming our belief that we are in fact *not* good enough to have close friends.

Beliefs come to us on their own. Few of us are consciously aware of choosing what we believe. Mary didn't sit down and "decide" to change her lifelong belief about men as mostly kind, helpful, interesting human beings. When she became aware of her post-traumatic belief *as a belief*— a mental construct that could take any shape at all—she said it was as if her belief about men changed all by itself. It didn't ask her permission; it just shape-shifted from a helpful to an unhelpful entity. When we experience childhood trauma, unhelpful beliefs oftentimes grow up with us, indivisible from our sense of self. As Chekhov noted, we might then (mistakenly) experience our worthlessness as being equally self-evident as our having two hands and feet. We fail to realize we are in fact not *what* we believe but the one *doing* the believing.

DISTORTION'S DARK POWER

When triggered by events around us, unhelpful beliefs give rise to negative thoughts that produce the panic, rage, and despair associated with PTSD. An essential feature of these negative thoughts is that they are always somewhat *distorted*. They are like fun house mirrors that reflect unreal pictures of ourselves, others, and the world. Like microscopic lenses they make what is small look huge. Like telescopic lenses they make what is far away look very near. It is this distortion of reality—and our *believing* these thoughts—that gives them power to terrorize, demoralize, and shame us.

This is exactly what happened to Abe. Abe did one tour of combat duty in Vietnam, then re-upped. In the midst of tremendous suffering on all sides he thought he might somehow help matters with his presence. Again and again, friendships he formed within his platoon or with Vietnamese civilians ended in his friends' violent deaths. When Abe finally returned to his family's ranch in Nebraska he had acquired a new belief: *Anyone I get close to likely will die or go away.* He spoke with his father who reinforced this idea telling Abe, "Yes, some people are just strange attractors of the grim reaper." Now Abe's thinking began to change. When he met a potential friend he'd tell himself *I should protect this person and myself by not getting too close.*

Abe's thought is an example of a distortion called "telescopy." Here we view the world as through a telescope that collapses space and time. It's true that we will, finally, be separated from everyone we know. We acknowledge this fact even in our marriage ceremonies: *Until death do us part.* Not *Unless* death do us part. *Until.* After Vietnam Abe saw death as the central, imminent characteristic of all relationships. Formerly very social, he started keeping to himself, all the while feeling lonely, depressed, and dissatisfied with his increasingly solitary existence.

Mary's thought about her fellow student, *He's going to follow me home,* contains a different distortion, which is called "clairvoyance." Here Mary is telling herself she can read people's thoughts (as well as the future). Clairvoyance is always present when we're feeling anxious. At such moments we're telling ourselves some version of the thought *I have seen the future and it is bad.* We might be in a very dangerous situation—for example, a military firefight—but if we're not channeling the clairvoyant we will not experience anxiety. Such is the power of thought. Much more than our physical surroundings, negative thinking is what produces our emotional suffering.

Another common distortion is the "judge." As judge we set

ourselves up as the final authority on the way things are. Judge thoughts often contain the word "should." *He should do this. She shouldn't do that. The world should/shouldn't,* and so on. Often we'll sit in judgment on ourselves: *I shouldn't feel this way. I should just be able to do this.* At the end of a long life of clinical work the German psychoanalyst Karen Horney wrote about the "tyranny of the shoulds." She concluded that all the emotional suffering she'd treated arose from one of three judge statements: *I should . . . You should . . . The world should . . .* Our own work with trauma survivors suggests Horney was seeing a deep truth.

A distortion called "microscopy" oftentimes shows up in negative thoughts that produce feelings of worthlessness and shame. At kindergarten age, Trissa was fondled by her older sister. Trissa loved and looked up to her sister, and after being sexually abused she could find no easy place for this experience in the big picture of her life. As a result these moments from early childhood continued to command her attention, becoming a center around which she arranged the rest of her life. *People want to take advantage of me,* she'd tell herself, experiencing this one hard fact as her entire life story. She grew up wary of anyone who expressed an interest in her. Though many approached her with kindness and respect, Trissa lived her relational life on edge, always waiting for the other shoe to drop.

There are dozens of ways we distort our thinking. The "mirror" is a distortion in which we see ourselves as the cause of any bad thing that happens. If someone is angry, unhappy, or rejecting, we immediately own this as *our* doing, our fault.

"Truthiness," a term coined by Stephen Colbert, refers to our believing "a gut feeling" while ignoring all data to the contrary. Though all external signs point to a particular thing being a certain way, we "just know" that something quite different is the case. Truthiness often takes the presence of some emotion as "proof" of some proposition. "I wouldn't be so scared if I *weren't* in real danger," we say. While this formulation gets things exactly backward, it can feel tremendously compelling and true.

A clue to identifying any distortion is the negative emotion it produces. Anger points toward the judge. Fear points to clairvoyance. Guilt and shame often arise from mirroring. Just as we each have distinct fingerprints, we each distort our thinking in a particular way. By gaining awareness of our individual habits of mind, we can more quickly recognize distorted thinking that offers itself to us and make a good decision whether to invest in it or not.

NO GOOD DEED UNPUNISHED

It's an unkind fact that oftentimes the very best people among us—the kindest, most sociable, and most loving of us all—fall prey to PTSD. Abe is a good example. Others in his unit seemed far less touched by the suffering around them. Or they numbed themselves with drugs and displays of braggadocio. Some actually seemed happiest when inflicting suffering on others. Not Abe. He always felt others' suffering as his own. While many died around him and Abe soldiered on, he began having a recurring nightmare. He'd dream he was at a funeral. When it came his turn to file by the coffin to pay his respects he'd startle awake in a cold sweat. It was Abe himself lying dead in the casket.

We'll return to this topic in chapter 4, "The Hidden Wisdom of Symptoms." Viewing PTSD symptoms—nightmares, flashbacks, rage, or despair—only as manifestations of psychopathology misses an essential truth. Almost always these symptoms express something fundamental about us, about the values we hold dear, about the very core of our humanity. Abe had never felt entirely separate from the people around him. And so it makes sense that a comrade's death would register, even in his dreams, as his own death. After the war, sitting alone at the fishing pond on his family's ranch in Nebraska, Abe would be startled by the screams of those dying beside him. There was no one left but Abe to grieve their passing. And a deep, deep part of him did not want ever to turn away from these last moments of his dying friends.

HAPPY *HOMO SAPIENS*

Metacognition, the ability to think about thinking, distinguishes our species. It's due to this skill that we call ourselves *Homo sapiens,* "wise people." Other primates are capable of simple thought but only humans are aware of the act of thinking itself. So it's no surprise that from the start the human record notes the relationship between thinking and the rest of life.

Interestingly this record regularly reports an inverse relationship between thinking and human happiness. A twelfth-century account of Buddha's enlightenment quotes the sage as having exclaimed that all people are already enlightened, "Yet simply because of their delusions and preoccupations they cannot bear witness to this endowment."[1] The Greek Stoic philosophers wrote at length about how thinking drives human suffering. Arrian, a second-century disciple of the Stoic philosopher Epictetus, quoted his teacher in his short manual of Stoic advice, *The Enchiridion:* "Men are disturbed not by what happens to them, but by the principles and notions they form concerning what happens to them."

Our ability to think thus seems a mixed blessing. The human brain's prefrontal cortex secretes thoughts just as the pancreas secretes insulin and the adrenals secrete adrenaline. Nature has selected for these mechanisms because they help us live well and pass on our genes to the next generation. Our ability to plan, for example, can help ensure our survival. But what of Mary's plan to stay safe by avoiding men at school? Mary seemed less to be *using* cognition than being *used by* it—a state of affairs that always leads to emotional distress and a smaller life. How can we learn to *use* this unique capacity and to minimize *being used* by it?

Marcus Tullius Cicero provided a clue in *Tusculanae Disputationes* (Tusculan Questions). "A bad feeling is a commotion of the mind," wrote Cicero, "repugnant to reason and against nature." Let's focus on the second part of this statement: *repugnant to reason and against nature.*

According to Cicero unhealthy negative emotion is driven by something entirely unnatural. We do not find depression, bitterness, or suicidal tendencies in nature. These are inventions of the human mind. So too human "reason"—thinking that is *reasonable,* that accords with the way things are—will not produce "commotion of the mind." In the same way the healthy human body responds to its environment in adaptive ways, the healthy human mind responds with adaptive thinking to whatever befalls us. Reason, we might say, is the cognitive expression of our innate naturalness.

Emperor Marcus Aurelius, a follower of Zeno of Citium, the accepted founder of Stoicism, wrote in his *Meditations,* "Everything that happens happens as it should." Aurelius's statement hoists the tyranny of the *shoulds* on their own petard. All that occurs *should* occur. It is only our delusions and preoccupations, our distorted negative thoughts and feelings, that prevent us from seeing this is so.

The thirteenth-century Dominican Meister Eckhart took this position a step further. Eckhart taught that *Wirklischkei* (reality) and *Gottheit* (divinity) are not separate. Reality perfectly expresses not only our human nature but divine will as well. When we realize and embody this truth we, like the Buddha, attain enlightenment. Or in Christian terms, we go to heaven. "The kingdom of God is within you," Jesus told his followers. When we see things clearly we realize heaven is where we've always been. Heaven is not somewhere else or some other time: it is the structure of reality itself.

Kundalini master Yogi Bhajan, who taught the yoga practices presented in this book, told his students, "Happiness is your birthright."[2] He, too, understood the perennial wisdom: we are already whole and happy, however else we are. The problem is we distract ourselves from this prior reality, allowing unhelpful beliefs and negative thinking to hijack our experience of living and dying. Oftentimes our patients tell us, "My problem is I overthink things." We like to remind them of the advice attributed to Ted Williams, legendary left-fielder for the Boston Red Sox: "If you don't think too good, don't think too much."

Well enough! But how can we learn to think less when we're already not thinking too good? How can millennia of accumulated wisdom help Mary in the midst of a panic attack during computer class? Or help Abe, waking for the thousandth time from the nightmare of seeing himself lying dead in a pine box? *Intellectual* knowledge of the rightness of the way things are won't help us in our most terrible moments of anguish and distress. Such moments require another kind of knowing, a direct experience of wellness that arises from the core of our being.

The following chapters will teach you how to locate this certainty at the center of your own body and mind.

Note: Before reading further please obtain a notebook in which to record our work together. We will do many experiments along the way and having a lab book in which to record the data they produce will be an important part of your recovery. You can think of this book as your recovery diary. Before making an entry, write the day's date so that we also have a longitudinal record of our work.

2

Embodied Stress

Trauma's aftereffects have been recognized for thousands of years. A cuneiform tablet from the Sumerian Third Dynasty (2100 BCE) describes the aftermath of a war in Mesopotamia in which civilians suffered panic and insomnia, and wept "bitter tears."[1] The fourth-century BCE Greek tragedian Sophocles, himself a soldier, wrote the play *Ajax,* in which the eponymous hero returns from the Trojan War a disordered veteran showing classic PTSD symptoms. Ajax eventually kills himself in an attempt to escape his mental anguish. World War I brought "shell shock" into the lexicon and World War II gave us "battle fatigue"—terms describing these same centuries-old forms of post-traumatic suffering.

In the past thirty years scientists have been studying these symptoms right down to the molecular level. In the late 1980s PTSD-related hormonal changes were first measured. In the 1990s, scanning technology allowed observation of PTSD-related structural and functional changes in the brain. We now know the effects of PTSD reach far beyond psychological disturbance, affecting many parts of the nervous system and immune function as well.

Now the good news: New research demonstrates cognitive behavioral therapy, yoga, and meditation can *reverse* many trauma-related changes in the brain and body. The tools you'll learn in this book will help you do precisely this. Before moving on to the tools themselves we'll first present an overview of how different parts of the brain and body are affected by trauma and the ways in which yoga and CBT can counteract these changes.

BRAIN STRUCTURES IMPLICATED IN PTSD

Amygdala

The amygdala is comprised of a pair of almond-shaped structures—the amygdalae—located on each side of the brain (see figure 2.1). The amygdala plays a key role in the regulation of traumatic memories and of general emotional processing. It is involved in *fear conditioning,*

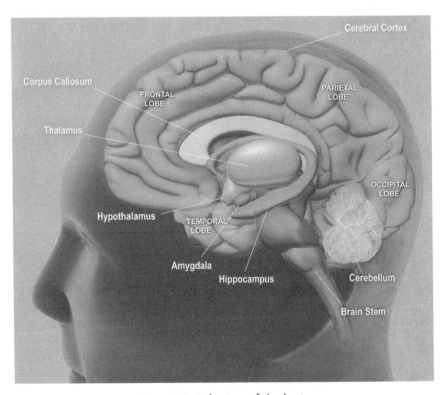

Figure 2.1. Side view of the brain
Image courtesy of the National Institute on Aging/
National Institutes of Health

a term that refers to the process by which fear is triggered by events around us. Post-traumatic changes in the amygdala may account for the hypervigilance associated with PTSD.[2]

The amygdala is overactive in people with PTSD. The left and right amygdalae have slightly different functions: the left amygdala is involved in a more detailed processing of emotion that involves thinking; the right processes emotion in a more automatic way.[3] The right amygdala shows increased activation in PTSD.[4]

Meditation reduces overactivation of the amygdala. Chanting *Om* has been shown to decrease activation of the right amygdala.[5] Participants in an eight-week mindfulness-meditation program had significant deactivation of the right amygdala when they were shown emotionally charged images.[6] These meditation studies on the amygdala were done in healthy volunteers. Such studies have not been done with PTSD patients but have been done using CBT protocols. Results showed CBT treatment also resulted in reductions in amygdala activity.[7]

Hippocampus

The word "hippocampus" comes from the Greek word for seahorse, due to this brain structure's resemblance to that creature. We have two hippocampi, one on each side of the brain (see figure 2.1). The hippocampus stores new memories, processes long-term memory, and appears to interact with the amygdala during the encoding of emotional memories. Because studies of laboratory animals under extreme stress show both damage to the hippocampus and memory impairment, hippocampus damage is believed to play a role in PTSD memory disturbances.[8]

The hippocampus is reduced in size in those with PTSD. Several studies have found that a smaller hippocampus correlates with more severe PTSD symptoms. In order to determine whether PTSD causes the hippocampus to shrink or if in fact people with a smaller hippocampus are more prone to develop PTSD, a study was done in forty pairs of male twins; in each pair, one was a Vietnam combat veteran and the other had no combat exposure. The results of this study suggest that a smaller hippocampus may make one vulnerable to developing PTSD, rather than PTSD causing the hippocampus to shrink.[9] However, if a smaller hippocampus was a risk factor for PTSD we would expect people with either current or past PTSD to have a smaller hippocampus. This was not the case in a study of Gulf War veterans; those who recovered from PTSD actually had a larger hippocampus.[10] This may be due to the ability of the hippocampus to generate new nerve cells and increase in size.

Yoga, meditation, and CBT all increase hippocampal volume, often rather quickly. Studies of mindfulness meditation showed significant hippocampus increases after just eight weeks.[11] Yoga has also been shown to increase the size of the hippocampus in older people after six months of yoga practice.[12] Twelve weeks of CBT have been found to increase the size of the hippocampus and improve memory in people with PTSD.[13]

Anterior Cingulate Cortex

The anterior cingulate cortex (ACC) is located in the front part of the cingulate cortex, which enwraps the corpus callosum that connects the two sides of the brain. The ACC regulates emotion and the stress response. It is involved in behavioral inhibition and fear conditioning.[14] Trauma may degrade the ACC's ability to regulate the amygdala, resulting in an enhanced fear response to PTSD triggers.[15]

The ACC is altered in both size and activity in PTSD. Vietnam veterans with PTSD were found to have decreased ACC activity compared to veterans without PTSD.[16] The ACC is also physically smaller in the brains of people who have been exposed to trauma as compared to those not so exposed.[17] The results from the Vietnam veteran twins study showed that reduced size of the ACC is most likely due to trauma, as opposed to being a predisposing factor in developing PTSD.[18]

Both CBT and meditation can reverse changes to the ACC found in PTSD. ACC thickness was increased in Zen meditators and the increase in thickness correlated to years of practice: those with more meditation experience had a thicker ACC.[19] Mindfulness meditation also resulted in increased activation of the ACC in experienced meditators.[20] Increased ACC activation was found following CBT treatment as well, and correlated with a decrease in PTSD symptoms.[21]

Table 2.1. Effect of Trauma on the Brain and the Healing Role of Yoga, Meditation, and CBT

Region of Brain	Functions	Effect of Trauma	Effect of Yoga, Meditation, and CBT
Amygdala	• Regulation of the memory of traumatic events • Emotional processing	Overactivation	Meditation and CBT decrease activity
Hippocampus	• Stores new memories • Processes long-term memory	Decreased size	Yoga, meditation, and CBT increase size
Anterior Cingulate Cortex	• Regulates the stress response • Regulates emotions • Inhibits behavior • Modulates fear conditioning	Decreased size and activity	Meditation increases size and activity; CBT increases activity

PHYSIOLOGIC EFFECTS OF PTSD

PTSD changes not only the body's structure but its function as well. Trauma affects activity in many systems in the body including the nervous, endocrine, and immune systems.

Neurotransmitter Production

Gamma-aminobutyric acid (GABA) is the main inhibitory neurotransmitter in the brain and is found in the blood as well. GABA reduces electrical signals in nerve cells, which has a calming effect on the whole person.

PTSD patients have decreased levels of GABA in both brain and blood.[22] Pharmacological agents such as benzodiazepines increase GABA and reduce PTSD symptoms.

Yoga has also been found to increase GABA levels in the brain, and this can happen very quickly. In one study, one hour of yoga practice increased practitioners' brain GABA levels 27 percent. Comparison subjects who read a book for one hour had no change in GABA levels.[23] Another study found increases in GABA after twelve weeks of yoga practice that correlated with improved mood and decreased anxiety.[24]

The Nervous System and Heart Rate Variability

Earlier we looked at the sympathetic and parasympathetic branches of the nervous system. The sympathetic nervous system is associated with arousal and the parasympathetic nervous system with relaxation (figure 2.2, page 21).

One measure of the balance between these sides of the nervous system is heart rate variability. Heart rate variability is the variation in the time interval between heartbeats. High heart rate variability is healthy and suggests that the parasympathetic nervous system is dominating. Low heart rate variability is unhealthy and indicates that the sympathetic nervous system is dominating.

Given the high state of arousal in PTSD it is not surprising to find it associated with low heart rate variability.[25] Low heart rate variability may also be a predisposing factor to developing PTSD.[26] Yoga has been shown to increase heart rate variability.[27] Studies also show CBT produces heart rate variability changes in women with PTSD.[28]

Sympathetic System

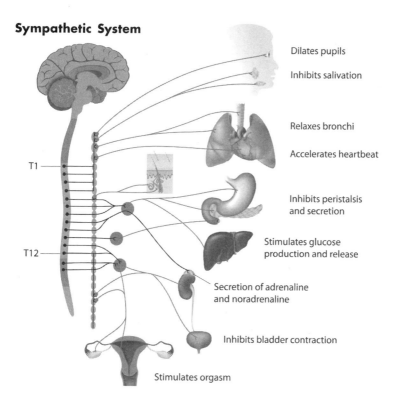

Dilates pupils

Inhibits salivation

Relaxes bronchi

Accelerates heartbeat

Inhibits peristalsis and secretion

Stimulates glucose production and release

Secretion of adrenaline and noradrenaline

Inhibits bladder contraction

Stimulates orgasm

T1

T12

Parasympathetic System

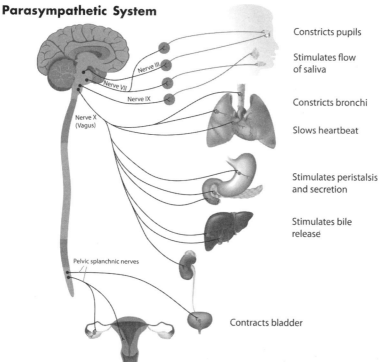

Constricts pupils

Stimulates flow of saliva

Constricts bronchi

Slows heartbeat

Stimulates peristalsis and secretion

Stimulates bile release

Contracts bladder

Nerve III

Nerve VII

Nerve IX

Nerve X (Vagus)

Pelvic splanchnic nerves

Figure 2.2. Two Branches of the Nervous System
Image courtesy of alila ©123RF.com

Allostatic Load

Our bodies are hardwired to respond to emergencies. The human stress response releases the hormones adrenaline and cortisol to shut down physical systems not needed in an emergency. When the emergency has passed, our bodies are designed to reset to baseline. This system works very well in the short-term and can indeed save our lives. But repeated attempts to adapt to chronic stressors have a cumulative negative effect on our bodies known as "allostatic load."[29] Allostatic load is measured by such biological markers as blood pressure, cholesterol, stress hormones, and blood sugar levels. Mothers with PTSD whose children had been diagnosed with cancer had trauma symptoms directly related to allostatic load; those with the highest levels of PTSD symptoms also had the highest allostatic loads.[30]

Insomnia, a common PTSD symptom, is another stressor that contributes to allostatic load. Four months of CBT produced decreased disease biomarkers in insomnia patients.[31] Studies have not yet measured the effect of yoga on allostatic load, but we know that yoga improves factors associated with allostatic load. As noted above yoga increases GABA and increases parasympathetic dominance as measured by increased heart rate variability. Yoga also decreases stress hormone production.[32] When PTSD increases allostatic load, CBT and yoga reduce and repair the wear and tear on the body, returning us to a balanced state.

CBT has been shown to regulate the stress response even at the level of gene expression. FKBP5 is a gene that plays a role in modulating the stress response. Although the expression of this gene is reduced when there is PTSD, twelve weeks of CBT was found to increase the expression of FKBP5 in study participants with PTSD.[33]

Inflammation

Inflammation is a protective response to tissue injury, microbial infection, and irritants, but when inflammation is out of control it can cause damage to healthy tissue. Inflammation is associated with many diseases including heart disease, diabetes, arthritis, osteoporosis, Alzheimer's, and cancer. It is regulated by proteins called cytokines, which can be either pro-inflammatory or anti-inflammatory. Levels of these cytokines in the blood indicate the degree of inflammation in the body. PTSD is associated with a pro-inflammatory state as a result of an increase in pro-inflammatory cytokines and a decrease in anti-inflammatory cytokines.[34]

Yoga practice returns the body to a healthy cytokine balance by decreasing pro-inflammatory cytokines and increasing anti-inflammatory cytokines.[35] CBT has also been shown to decrease pro-inflammatory cytokines in the blood after only seven weeks of treatment.[36] Just as CBT has been shown to regulate genes associated with the stress response, both yoga and CBT regulate inflammatory genes. Reduced inflammation-related gene expression was found in people practicing a meditation from Kundalini Yoga as taught by Yogi Bhajan®[37] similar to the meditation taught in chapter 9 in this book. Comparable results were seen in women with breast cancer who participated in a different yoga program.[38] Women with breast cancer who received CBT after surgery also had a significant down-regulation of the genes that code for pro-inflammatory cytokines.[39]

Telomeres

Telomeres are protective DNA sequences at the tips of chromosomes that serve to stabilize them. As we age, telomeres shorten. Shortened telomeres are associated with several diseases including diabetes, heart disease, and cancer. Telomere shortening may result from increased sympathetic nervous system activity, inflammation, oxidation, and certain stress hormones. Emerging evidence suggests that telomeres are also shortened in those with PTSD.[40] Yoga may help preserve telomere length. There is a strong genetic variant involved in telomere maintenance, but longer telomeres have also been found in yoga practitioners with at least two years of practice compared to a sedentary group.[41]

Table 2.2. Effect of Trauma
on the Autonomic Nervous System,
the Endocrine System, and the Immune System
and the Healing Role of Yoga, Meditation, and CBT

System	Healthy Status	Effect of Trauma	Effect of Yoga, Meditation, and CBT
Autonomic Nervous System: Heart Rate Variability	High heart rate variability (parasympathetic dominance)	Low heart rate variability (sympathetic dominance)	Yoga and CBT increase heart rate variability
Endocrine System and Autonomic Nervous System: Stress Response and Allostatic Load	Low stress levels/ low allostatic load	Increased stress levels/high allostatic load	Yoga improves factors involved in allostatic load; CBT reduces allostatic load
Immune System: Inflammation	Balance of pro-inflammatory cytokines	Increased pro-inflammatory cytokines and decreased anti-inflammatory cytokines	Yoga and CBT decrease pro-inflammatory cytokines and increase anti-inflammatory cytokines
Endocrine System, Autonomic Nervous System, and Immune System: Telomere Length	Healthy telomere length	Shortened telomeres	Yoga supports healthy telomere length

RESEARCH ON CBT, YOGA, AND PTSD

Randomized controlled trials (RCTs) are considered the gold standard in research. These studies compare a treatment group with a control group that did not receive the treatment protocol. Many RCTs have shown CBT to be an effective PTSD treatment. An RCT using Kundalini Yoga as taught by Yogi Bhajan, as presented in this book, found that participants in an eight-week program had significantly decreased PTSD symptoms, improved sleep, less perceived stress, more positive mood, greater resilience, and less anxiety compared to a control group that did not participate in the program.[42] Participants reported other benefits[43] including:

1. Enhanced calmness, stability, hope, and balance
2. Greater control of thought patterns and mental clarity
3. More confidence, self-esteem, motivation, determination, and resilience

Improvements in PTSD symptoms have been measured in studies of various yoga styles. One of these studies was an RCT and others were pilot studies.[44] Studies containing elements of yoga such as mantra, mindfulness meditation, and yogic breathing have all shown improvement in PTSD symptoms.[45] Our pilot study of the CBT and yoga techniques presented in this book showed significant improvements in overall PTSD symptoms and in all four PTSD symptom clusters: intrusion, arousal, avoidance, and negative alterations in mood.[46] Participants also experienced significant improvements in sleep and most improvements were maintained two months following the end of the program.

When patients start using the tools we teach in this book, often their lives change—not only in the moment but for months and years afterward. Any benefit received from taking a medication likely ends when the pill is no longer taken. When we reset our bodies and minds with CBT and yoga, our bodies and minds tend to stay reset to a new normal that is very different from the anguished days and nights that are the hallmark of PTSD. The next chapters will show you how to begin running the experiments and collecting the data that will enable you to make this healing reset for yourself.

3

Cognitive-Behavioral
Therapy

Cognitive-behavioral therapy (CBT) is a twentieth-century American science of the mind. Its roots go back millennia to the teachings of spiritual masters including the Buddha and philosophers such as Zeno of Citium. CBT has used this ancient wisdom to help develop real-world tools to place in the hands of people suffering from PTSD and other forms of emotional anguish. This chapter will provide an overview of how CBT works and introduce the first tools you can pick up and immediately put to use in your own life.

THE SCIENTIFIC METHOD

We trace modern Western science back to a brilliant cadre of eleventh-century Arab physicists, astronomers, and physicians. These investigators followed a similar pattern of inquiry that formed the basis of what we know today as the scientific method. CBT adopts this approach and invites patients to become investigators of themselves, running experiments in the laboratories of their own bodies and minds. There are a number of components of this method. Let's review them now.

Observation

The first component is *observation*. It involves collecting information about ourselves and the world through our senses, our interactions with others, and our experiences of acting and noticing the consequences of our actions. What is the difference between experience and observation? As you are reading this sentence you are experiencing something physical that it is unlikely you are also observing. After the colon in this sentence you will be observing it: sensation in the sole of your left foot.

What happened when you read that last phrase? What happened is the first step of the scientific method and of CBT. Instead of simply *being* your experience you became an observer of it. All day every day we experience things: physical sensations, emotions, and thought patterns. Most of our experience we fail to observe. While *having* an experience we don't *notice* it. While this is well and good when it comes to sensation in our feet or many other aspects of living, failure to observe certain parts of our physical, emotional, and cognitive experience can contribute to the development and maintenance of symptoms associated with PTSD.

A patient named Diana was merging onto an interstate when an eighteen-wheeler abruptly changed lanes, pinning her compact car against a concrete retaining wall. Diana survived the shower of sparks and breaking glass without serious physical injury but shortly thereafter began feeling panicked when she approached interstate on-ramps. We accompanied her on a drive and saw that, unbeknownst to her, a half-mile before the interstate Diana's respiration changed. She began breathing more shallowly and quickly, a behavior that removes more carbon dioxide from the blood than usual. This raised her blood's alkalinity, causing Diana to feel dizzy. Her heart began to palpitate and her hands to tingle. By the time she'd arrived at the on-ramp she'd primed herself to have a full-blown panic attack.

Another patient, Matías, had lost his younger sister to suicide fifteen years earlier. Matías felt angry and depressed. His sister had died over the Christmas holidays and each year this was a particularly difficult time for Matías. As he himself had a good life, a loving wife, and a job he liked, Matías believed he had no reason to be unhappy. "Perhaps it's a brain imbalance," he told himself, and tried antidepressant medication. It didn't help. Then Matías read about PTSD and came to us for an evaluation.

We asked Matías to tell us about the content of his thinking. At first he didn't know what we meant, so we explained to him the concept of metacognition and asked him to begin observing and writing down his thoughts. This was a new idea for Matías. While he'd experienced thinking his entire life he'd never removed himself from it enough to observe it. When he did so he was shocked by what he saw. All day every day, just below the level of conscious awareness, he was telling himself *I should have known Maria was so desperate. I shouldn't have left her alone that weekend. She always looked to me for protection. It's my fault she died.*

Like many of our patients, Matías was aware of his negative emotion but not the thinking that was producing it. Bringing this cognition into awareness was the first step in his coming to terms with his sister's death and freeing himself from the chronic feelings of anger and depression he had lived with for so many years.

Sometimes emotion itself is what goes missing. Lei, a successful business professional, came to us complaining of failed relationships with men and general feelings of numbness. She described a traumatic childhood in which her parents demanded perfection from her, then beat her when (in their eyes) she fell short. Since leaving home Lei had done extraordinarily well in school and in her professional life. She continued to live close to her parents who, aging now, increasingly looked to her for assistance.

We offered Lei uncovering tools that led her down through her emotional numbness to a blind rage that lay beneath it. Lei was tremendously angry at both her parents, but because her culture placed a premium on respect for one's elders—and as Lei herself continued to value being "the perfect daughter"—she'd struck a bargain with herself not to observe this emotion. When she became angry with a man she was dating she struck the same deal. The end result was the chronic numbness and unsatisfying relational life that brought Lei to us for treatment.

Measurement

Science begins with observation and moves on to *measurement*. We might think of measurement as a more fine-grained type of observation. We can observe that a glass is filled with water. We might then measure the volume or purity of that fluid. Science always requires some means of measuring, of quantifying what is observed.

CBT regularly takes the measure of various aspects of life. We measure the intensity of emotions and the degree of belief in thoughts. We also quantify the frequency and duration of certain behaviors. Why?

Measurement sets an expectation of change and can motivate us to make that change. As children many of us had parents place a mark on a doorjamb recording our height. We expected that number to change year to year. For the same reason runners time their races, golfers measure their driving distance, pitchers clock the speed of their fastballs. When CBT assigns a number to something we cue a subconscious expectation that the number can and perhaps will change.

Measurement also scales data so we can compare moments across time. If we simply observe we are angry on Monday and again angry on Tuesday we might miss noticing important information. Perhaps we were 95 percent angry on Monday and 10 percent angry on Tuesday. If we were both observing *and measuring* this emotion we'd observe a significant shift. If this change occurred during a CBT experiment we might decide to continue the experiment and collect additional data on this emotion.

Measuring our degree of belief in a thought is another core component of CBT. We've seen how distortions in a negative thought give it power to create unhealthy negative emotion. What actualizes this power is our degree of belief in the thought. Consider the negative thought *The world is about to end.* Can you identify the distortions in this thought? These might include clairvoyance (ability to see the future) and telescopy (the world certainly *will* end, though probably not as soon as this thought suggests). If we are upset by this thought it's likely that we believe it, distortions and all. We might then also identify a secret judge sitting in this thought: *The world is about to end, but it shouldn't!* On the other hand, while thinking this distorted negative thought we may not be troubled at all. If so it's likely because we don't believe it—or believe it very little. If we believe such a thought 2 percent or 3 percent it might lend some momentary excitement to our lives, as might a science fiction movie about a giant asteroid at the Saturday matinee. But at 3 percent belief it's unlikely this thought will produce unhealthy negative feelings of panic, rage, or despair.

CBT also measures the occurrence of behaviors. After Mark was caught in the crossfire of two rival gangs downtown he began avoiding leaving his suburban home in the evenings. From one point of view this behavior makes perfect sense. Avoidance is so common after trauma that it is one of the criteria necessary for a diagnosis of PTSD. But for Mark this healthy instinct to protect himself became a snowballing problem of its own. Eventually Mark confined his public outings to the short drive between his home and office. When this outing too began feeling scary—as did answering the doorbell and even the phone—he reached out to us for help.

We gave Mark a small digital counter like the ones golfers wear on their wrists. We asked him to click it whenever he found himself avoiding exposure to the wider world, and then write his daily total for these behaviors on a log sheet. Along with the cognitive tools we offered Mark, observing, measuring, and recording his actual behavior on a daily basis became an important part of his therapy. It provided him all the benefits of measurement described above and kept us honest in evaluating the effectiveness of our work together.

Experiment

Experiment is the axle of all science. Designing and implementing a protocol and collecting data that supports or refutes a hypothesis is where scientific rubber meets the road. Human beings are inherently experimental. As children we are mad scientists constantly running experiments—doing things and seeing what happens. In scientific terms we manipulate an independent variable (do something) and then measure the response of a dependent variable (see what happens).

Experiments cannot fail. They either confirm some hypothesis or refute it. We'll offer you dozens of recovery tools in the pages ahead and explain how to set up your own experiments with them. If a particular tool helps you make a change you'd like to make, great! If another tool does not help at all, that's fine too. If tools are helpful you may want to continue to use them. Unhelpful tools you'll likely set down in order to pick up another. Only you can collect *your* data, and this data will always look a bit different from the data collected by anyone else.

When trauma crashes into our lives it can shut down our personal laboratories. We can lose our curiosity about things, or tell ourselves the data is all in for this lifetime. We lose our willingness to "do something" and our interest in "seeing what happens." Leaving behind our mad scientist we leave behind much that enlivens us and makes us prone to curiosity, joy, surprise, and an ever-deepening experience of life on earth.

The fact that you are reading these words suggests that while your mad scientist may have taken a long sabbatical, he or she is still willing to don a lab coat and collect some new data. Good for you! The *willingness* of thousands of trauma survivors we've helped heal has been the active ingredient in their recoveries. In scientific language willingness is the "catalyst" that activates the process of change. Without it there is only a low probability of healing. With it anything can happen, and regularly does.

So—let's roll up our sleeves and do some science!

EXPERIMENT 1

Cognition, Emotion, and Sensation

Step One: Get your lab book, date this entry, and sit in a comfortable chair. Close your eyes and imagine yourself in some very pleasant place. Perhaps you're at the beach on a summer day. Hear the seagulls calling and the waves rolling into shore. Or maybe you're sitting by a crackling fire in a mountain cabin in the snowy woods. Smell the wood smoke and feel the soft down comforter against your skin. After a minute or so rate how peaceful you are on a scale of 0 to 10. Here "0" would be not at all peaceful; "10" would be Dalai Lama levels of peace and equanimity. Rate also how relaxed you are physically, using the same scale. Open your eyes and write those two numbers in your lab book.

Step Two: Again close your eyes and now imagine yourself in some moderately stressful scene. Perhaps you're having an argument with a friend or family member. Or maybe you're stuck in traffic on a hot day, your car's air conditioner is broken, and you're running late for an important meeting. Hear the car horns, smell the exhaust, notice the engine temperature needle on your dashboard moving into red. After a minute or so, again rate how peaceful you are on a scale of 0 to 10. Also note how relaxed you are and write these numbers below the first set.

Congratulations! You've just conducted your first experiment. You manipulated an independent variable—your thought pattern—and collected data on two dependent variables—feelings of peacefulness and of physical relaxation. Let's now analyze the data. Are your two sets of numbers the same? Different? If different, how so?

Most of us find our first peacefulness and relaxation numbers higher than our second. How might we account for this difference, called *variance* in scientific language? Epictetus, the Greek Stoic, proposed a hypothesis: it's not what happens to us (sitting in a comfortable chair) but our "views and opinions" (we're at the beach; we're sitting in traffic) that determine how we feel both physically and emotionally. CBT agrees with this hypothesis. Thousands of randomized controlled trials have found exactly this result. Many studies have recorded not only subjective reports of internal states but also significant changes in biomarkers such as stress hormones in the bloodstream, heart rate variability, and skin conductance. These physical measures and others are exquisitely sensitive to changes in cognition and the emotions our thinking creates.

An overwhelming body of scientific data now supports Epictetus's hypothesis: it is indeed what we tell ourselves about any experience that gives it the emotional meaning it has in our lives.

Let's now look at another important aspect of cognitive science: motivation. We might be telling ourselves something that creates great emotional suffering, and continue to do so day after day. What might motivate us to make—and keep making—such a painful choice?

THE NEW ROOTS OF
HUMAN SUFFERING

In recent decades researchers have made great strides in understanding physical pain. Data they've collected upends many traditional ideas about this fundamental human experience. Mechanical, Newtonian notions of "pain receptors" and "pain circuits" in the brain have given way to a more complex and nuanced perspective. At the center of this new worldview are motivational factors. It now seems that we experience much of the physical pain we do because our brains calculate that this sensation is important to our overall security and survival. Pain protects us from potential damage, or motivates us to attend to and repair damage already done.

The idea that pain is less an involuntary reaction and more a decision the brain makes is difficult for those very brains to comprehend at first. Yet consider for a moment the very real experience of phantom limb pain. Theresa is a typical example. She lost her left forearm in a motorcycle accident, but for years following the crash she was awakened at night by a stabbing pain in her left hand, which had borne the brunt of her initial impact with the street. Many people experience such pain, all without any Newtonian structure in place to explain it. Or consider Rick's experience after being shot in the back during a firefight in Afghanistan. Rick didn't know he'd been hit until a field medic asked him about the source of the blood covering the lower part of his body. Rick received no pain medication yet experienced no pain from the wound until a dressing change two days later. Mechanical models of pain can't account for such cases. How might we begin to understand them?

Today researchers liken the perception of pain to visual perception. The visual cortex receives input from the retina, processes it, and produces output—an image in the mind's eye. Far from being a mechanical, Newtonian process, visual perception is heavily influenced by cognitive factors: expectation, intention, and belief. We see what we most "need" to see. A visual image expresses first the brain's understanding of what is important for the wellness and success of the whole organism, followed by the brain's decisions based on that understanding. In similar fashion the brain receives input from the body's *nociceptors*—sensory nerve cells—processes this input, and produces output that may or may not include the sensation of pain. As with vision, motivational factors play a huge role in creating this output.

What does this have to do with the PTSD symptoms of panic, anger, flashbacks, and exaggerated startle response? Our research and that of others suggests there is a process at work very like that described in the physical pain literature. The traumatized brain takes input from the world around us, processes it, and provides the output it considers most important for the wellness of the whole organism. We can see how this worked for Rick, the Afghanistan combat veteran. After returning to the United States he suffered tremendously each Fourth of July. The sound of exploding fireworks (*input*) in his big city triggered the same panic (*output*) he'd experienced in Afghanistan. That response was part of what brought him back alive from that war, albeit with a Purple Heart. His brain seemed to have decided that as this output had protected him once, it would protect him again. Perhaps it also calculated that a "false positive" misreading of present-day danger was an allowable price for Rick to pay for an increased chance of survival going forward.

This new understanding of human suffering, both physical and emotional, opens a door to treating it. Those of us working in the emerging field of integrative medicine have developed tools to reset the brain so that the same input, sometimes called a *trigger,* produces different output. We help patients do this reset and decrease or entirely eliminate PTSD symptoms. Brain scans and other physiologic data demonstrate that these tools reshape not only the content but also the actual physical structure of the brain! When it comes to many components of the brain we are, quite literally, what we think.

THE ROLE OF BEHAVIOR

Cognitive-behavioral therapy begins with *thinking* (cognition), then moves on to *doing* (behavior). It's by *acting* in new ways that, finally, we open the door to reclaiming our lives. Let's take a look at human behavior, beginning with the word itself.

The origins of the word *behave* lie in Old English and German compounds that denote how one "has" or "bears" or "carries" oneself. Our earliest behavior, then, relates to our physical carriage: our posture, muscle tonus (normal partial contraction), and breath. We can extend carriage to include the mental image we hold of ourselves—as happy, worthwhile people or as unhappy, worthless human beings. From this perspective cognition is mental behavior—what we *do* with the organ that is our brain. These first mental behaviors set the stage for all the physical acts that flow from them.

Our physical behavior provides extremely important input to our brains. Even more than external events, the event of our own behaviors is information the brain processes to produce such outputs as physiologic reaction and emotion. Let's look at two examples of this phenomenon.

Mary, the wilderness guide who returned to school, regularly left class early to avoid the possibility of interacting with her male classmates. Each time she did this her brain took note of two things: (1) her avoidance behavior and (2) her safe arrival home. Connecting these dots, her brain "learned" that avoidance produced safety. When Mary left class her brain produced the output of feelings of relief. If she lingered to catch something her professor was saying, her brain produced feelings of stress and anxiety. In both cases we can see how Mary's brain took the input of her actions and produced output it considered appropriate to the well-being of the entire organism.

Cynthia was mugged one night on the streets of a large city. Since being attacked, walking downtown in the evening had triggered feelings of panic. In working with Cynthia we taught her a new way of walking city sidewalks. Instead of staying to one side and moving out of the way of anyone approaching, she learned to walk down the center of the sidewalk, head erect, eyes focused on a point a block away. "Jeez!" a friend walking with her exclaimed one evening. "It's like Moses parting the Red Sea!" People approaching Cynthia sensed her self-assurance and stepped out of *her* way. More importantly, Cynthia's own brain took note of this new input and changed the output it had been delivering: her feelings of panic disappeared and she began *enjoying* walking in the evening in the newfound freedom and power of her body and mind.

EXPERIMENT II

ᔕ Behavior (Breath), Emotion, and Sensation

Step One: Get your lab book, date this entry, and sit comfortably erect on a chair or on a cushion on the ground. Measure on a 1–10 scale how peaceful and also how physically relaxed you feel. Write both numbers in your lab book.

Step Two: Begin breathing with shallow, rapid breaths into and out of your chest, perhaps twice per second. After a minute or so, re-rate on a 1–10 scale your feelings of peacefulness and relaxation.

Step Three: Again sit comfortably erect, breathe normally, and after a minute or so rate your peacefulness and relaxation.

Step Four: Let your breath drop down into your belly so that when you inhale your navel moves away from your spine, and when you exhale it moves back toward your spine. Your chest and shoulders are now not moving at all. We call this diaphragmatic breathing and it is one of the breath patterns we'll experiment with throughout this book. Slow your breath rate so that you are completing one cycle of inhalation/exhalation every ten seconds or so. After one minute, again rate your feelings of both peacefulness and relaxation.

Congratulations! You've completed your second experiment. Let's look at the data. Are your pre-post numbers the same? Different? If different, how so?

When we breathe rapidly, also known as hyperventilating, we induce changes in our bodies related to heart rate, blood pressure, and the carbon dioxide level in our bloodstream. These changes can trigger the brain's fight-or-flight response, as well as feelings of anxiety and stress. Diaphragmatic breathing, on the other hand, changes the same biomarkers in the opposite direction, and the changes induced by diaphragmatic breathing last for hours afterward, even after we return to our usual breath pattern. We do diaphragmatic breathing while asleep or in a state of deep relaxation.

Yogis have understood and used the power of breath for millennia. You too can begin to harness this simple, powerful tool in your daily life. In chapter 7, "Yoga: Embodied Wellness," we will teach you a number of breathing practices and other yogic tools (behaviors) you can put to immediate use. As with the CBT tools you'll learn, your experiments with these ancient breath practices will produce the data you need to evaluate their effectiveness in your own life.

4

The Hidden Wisdom of Symptoms

Far from being simply the troubling aftereffects of trauma, PTSD symptoms frequently express our core values, resourcefulness, and commitment to survival. Remember that our brains take any input they receive and create the output they determine to be most important to us, so when we develop PTSD, it is because our brains create these symptoms for good reasons. Let's look at a sample of these reasons, grouped under their particular symptom clusters.

Good Reasons to Feel Negative Emotion

Anger holds my perpetrator to account and expresses my sense of morality and justice.

Horror is my living memorial to the sanctity of human life.

Anxiety keeps me alert to new dangers.

Guilt expresses my willingness to accept some responsibility for what happened.

Rage keeps others at bay and makes me feel safer and more powerful.

Fear is realistic; the world is a dangerous place.

Good Reasons to Experience Intrusive Symptoms

Flashbacks help me evaluate the danger of my current situation relative to a past threat.

Nightmares are my subconscious mind's effort to resolve my trauma.

Good Reasons for Avoidance

Avoiding triggering situations protects me from anxiety or from being injured again.

Given what I've experienced, avoidance demonstrates wisdom.

Avoidance is a form of self-care.

Good Reasons to Be Hypervigilant

If I'm vigilant I will perceive new danger before it can hurt me.

Fight-or-flight primes my body to respond in a way that will protect me.

Good Reasons for Emotional Numbness

If I shut down my heart I won't feel pain.

Indifference protects me from further disappointment.

Given what I've experienced, positive feelings would be inappropriate.

Dissociation enables me to tolerate situations I otherwise couldn't.

Good Reasons for Social Isolation

People have proven untrustworthy.

I have nothing to offer.

I'm different from others; they could never understand or accept me.

Good Reasons to Identify with My Trauma

For better and for worse I am this experience; I'd not know who I was if I let it go.

My whole life is organized around this; I wouldn't know how to live without it.

Moving on would be disloyal to the memory of those my survival has left behind.

Does this list help you begin to understand *your* brain's rationale for producing such symptoms? This understanding is an essential first step to resetting the output your brain is currently providing. We'll now share with you a discovery tool that is a process designed to help drill down and identify your brain's rationale for producing PTSD symptoms.

EXPERIMENT III

ᕯ Discovering a Symptom's Hidden Wisdom

Step One: Take out your lab book, date this entry, and write down a symptom you'd like to analyze.

Step Two: Write beneath it all the benefits of having this symptom.

Step Three: Write down the good things these benefits say about you as a human being.

Figures 4.1–4.4 (pages 42–43) show how four of our patients used the discovery tool of Hidden Wisdom.

How did you do with your own discovery? Were you able to identify some benefits of your symptom and the nice things these benefits say about you? Sometimes recognizing the benefits of a troubling symptom can be challenging! If you find yourself getting stuck, you can approach the question in another way. Ask yourself what you would have to give up if this symptom suddenly vanished. For example: *If I were never again angry when I thought about being attacked, what else would go away?* Possible answers might include: my identity as a victim or survivor, my interest in blaming my perpetrator, a community of angry fellow victims, or pleasure in fantasizing about revenge.

SYMPTOM: *Anxiety*

Benefits:

1. *Keeps me alert and informed about my environment*
2. *Primes me to respond early on to potential threats*
3. *Reduces the risk I'll be blindsided as I was that night in the cabin*

Good things these benefits say about me:

1. *I care about my safety*
2. *I deserve protection*
3. *I learn from mistakes*
4. *I am willing to be proactive in regard to my well-being*

Figure 4.1. Alicia's Hidden Wisdom

SYMPTOM: *Isolation*

Benefits:

1. *Protects me from dangerous people*
2. *Reduces my stress*
3. *Protects others from my angry outbursts*
4. *Reduces the chances I'll hurt someone or I'll get hurt myself*

Good things these benefits say about me:

1. *I care about myself*
2. *I care about others*
3. *I'm smart enough to plan my life in a way that acknowledges my limits*

Figure 4.2. Benito's Hidden Wisdom

SYMPTOM: *Shame*

Benefits:

1. *Holds me accountable*

2. *Keeps me humble*

3. *Lets me atone for my mistakes*

Good things these benefits say about me:

1. *I'm willing to take responsibility for my part in things*

2. *I have clear moral standards*

3. *I'm not going to lie to myself and turn away from the reality of who I am and what I've done*

Figure 4.3. Santana's Hidden Wisdom

SYMPTOM: *Insomnia*

Benefits:

1. *Sleeping lightly I'll hear if someone breaks into my home*

2. *Sleeping lightly I'll have fewer nightmares*

3. *Daytime tiredness reminds me not to overextend myself*

Good things these benefits say about me:

1. *I'm determined never again to be a victim*

2. *I deserve to feel well and secure whether asleep or awake*

Figure 4.4. Gretchen's Hidden Wisdom

You might also struggle to find the good things a particular benefit says about you as a human being. It may help to ask yourself: How does this benefit express my core values and beliefs? What does it say about how I care for myself and others? How does this benefit reflect my moral code and sense of justice?

Using the Hidden Wisdom tool, many of our patients begin to experience a fundamental shift in perception. Instead of seeing symptoms solely as problems or defects, they begin to appreciate the wisdom these symptoms embody. Often this leads to patients being more compassionate with themselves, and to reductions in feelings of shame, defectiveness, and inferiority. The traumatized brain is actually pretty smart! Even when producing troubling symptoms it does amazing work promoting what it sees as the deep self-interests of the person who is feeding and housing it, and thus keeping it alive.

PRICE IT

When we go into a store our brains become real-time calculators of price and benefit. When we examine an item of clothing or a kitchen appliance we weigh its price against the benefit we believe it will bring. If the benefit is greater than the price, we may purchase the item; if not, we'll likely not buy it.

Precisely this reckoning is the next step in evaluating the wisdom the Hidden Wisdom tool reveals. Once we've identified the benefits of a symptom and the ways in which it expresses our core values, we can consider the symptom's cost. In addition we'll add a numeric component to the equation to quantify and further clarify our perception of value. One number will express the appeal of the benefits, the other the weight of the price. Each will be a number between 0 and 100. We can think of the price number as units of payment, the benefit number as units of value.

See figure 4.5 for how Alicia priced anxiety and figure 4.6 (page 46) for how Benito priced isolating himself from others.

SYMPTOM: *Anxiety*	
Benefits of Being Anxious	***Price I Pay***
1. *Keeps me alert and informed about my environment*	1. *Feels terrible*
	2. *Disconnects me from others*
	3. *Keeps my life small*
2. *Primes me to respond early on to potential threats*	4. *Damages my physical heath*
	5. *Robs me of joy*
3. *Reduces the risk I'll be blindsided as I was that night in the cabin*	
25	**95**

Figure 4.5. Alicia's price

After pricing the personal cost, Alicia was shocked at the poor bargain she'd been making with herself for many years. Her "seat-of-the-pants" impression was that the benefits of anxiety represented a good bargain. However, after calculating the pricing she became angry at having cheated herself for so long, and her desire to crush her anxiety and relinquish its benefits became quite strong. Alicia was now a candidate for CBT. She quickly reset her brain's output (anxiety) using the tools we next taught her and began to reclaim a life of peace, joy, and connection with others.

Benito made the opposite decision. The emotional price he paid for physical/social/legal safety seemed a reasonably good bargain. Benito

SYMPTOM: Isolation	
Benefits of Isolation	***Price I Pay***
1. *Protects me from*	1. *Loneliness*
dangerous people	2. *Boredom*
2. *Reduces my stress*	3. *Lower self-esteem*
3. *Protects others from*	
my angry outbursts	
4. *Reduces the chances*	
I'll hurt someone or	
I'll get hurt myself	
70	*15*

Figure 4.6. Benito's price

decided he didn't want our help with this particular symptom at this time, so our work with him went in another direction.

EXPERIMENT IV

& Price It

Step One: Take out your lab book, date this entry, and write down any symptom you'd like to price.

Step Two: Itemize beneath it all the benefits of having this symptom.

Step Three: Itemize next the price you pay to get these benefits.

Step Four: Add a number at the end of each list.

Step Five: Calculate your value.

How does your pricing structure look? As Alicia did, are you purchasing benefits at too high a price? Or do some benefits look like a good bargain, as Benito found? Before reading further, complete this exercise to determine which PTSD symptoms you might want to crush and which you'd prefer to leave in place at this time. There are no right or wrong answers. Some shoppers purchase a particular item in a store, whereas others replace the item and keep shopping. You are the only one who can or should make such determinations about your symptoms.

Once pricing has helped you identify PTSD symptoms you're ready to leave behind, the next chapter of this book will teach you tools to do just that—walk away from habits of body and mind that have outworn their usefulness and no longer represent a good bargain in the big picture of your life.

5

Rewire Your Brain

The past thirty years have seen an explosion in research on "neuroplasticity," the brain's ability to remake itself following physical and emotional injury. We now know that like other parts of the body, the brain has a tremendous capacity to heal itself. The tools in this and the following chapters have helped many, many of our patients rewire their brains and produce the new output—thoughts, emotions, behaviors—they most want to live with in the future.

Before continuing, let's notice that there are two options available to us, symptom reduction and symptom elimination. Here are examples of each:

Remember Diana, the woman who survived a collision with a truck, then went on to develop panic attacks when entering expressways? Diana wanted help with her panic. She also told us it wouldn't feel right to completely eliminate her fear in such situations. We asked her for a number between 1 and 100—with 100 being a full-blown panic attack—that would feel like the right amount of fear to feel when merging onto an expressway. She came up with the number 15, which she felt would keep her alert and oriented in this potentially dangerous setting, yet not create unnecessary suffering and impaired judgment or reaction times. We thought this sounded like a perfect number, and 15 percent fear became the goal of our work with Diana.

Decades after having been attacked as a teenager, Alicia remained on high alert, her body and mind constantly in a state of fight-or-flight. In some way this felt right for her—"normal" was the word she used. After pricing her anxiety and finding she was paying three times more than what she was receiving in benefits, she became angry at having ripped herself off for so long! Alicia wanted to completely crush this chronic anxiety for the rest of her life. This kind of fear produced no benefit she could not acquire in other ways, and produced enormous downsides in her life. We told Alicia 0 percent anxiety sounded like a perfect number, and this became our goal.

Keep this "scaling" in mind as we move forward. There are no right or wrong ways to scale a symptom. The choice is yours alone and whatever choice you make will be the right one for you.

THE NEW DEAL

A first step to reducing or eliminating a symptom is a cognitive reset we call the "New Deal." We've seen how our brains strike deals, paying the price of a symptom in order to obtain the benefits it provides. Remember Rick, the veteran who suffered greatly each Fourth of July when fireworks triggered the same fight-or-flight response that had helped keep him safe during firefights in Afghanistan? Back home Rick's brain had concluded that a potential "false positive" reading of danger was an allowable price to pay for a life potentially saved. Rick himself was not happy with this arrangement. Dreading the buildup to the holiday and drinking heavily the day itself did not square with Rick's idea of the civilian life he wanted for himself and his family. So we helped him to renegotiate a new deal with his brain. Rick did this by first writing down each of the benefits the old deal was providing him and then "talking back" to this old way of doing business. Albert Ellis, one of the founders of CBT, called such backtalk "disputing." Disputation is a core element in CBT's toolbox. See figure 5.1 (page 50), Rick's New Deal worksheet.

SYMPTOM: *Flashbacks*
Benefits:
1. Might again save my life: I'll never know when an explosion might be the sign of danger
2. Reminds me and others of my status as a Purple Heart recipient and a wounded warrior
3. Gives me a reason to avoid people
4. Elicits concern and sympathy from my wife
Backtalk:
1. Now that I'm retired, panic has a very low chance of protecting me. It might actually shorten my life by stressing me out and giving me heart problems.
2. Everybody knows about my military service. It would now be more honorable to be a fully functioning member of my family and community.
3. If I don't want to be around people I can just say so. I don't need an excuse.
4. I would rather have my wife love me for just being me, as I love her just for being herself. That would be better for both of us and for our marriage.

Figure 5.1. Rick's New Deal

Can you see how Rick went back to the bargaining table with his brain? Our brains are, happily, always willing to renegotiate. After all, they want wellness as much as we do! So we're not sitting across the table from our brains as opponents. Rather we're sitting side by side as we look for a new way to reassemble the puzzle pieces in front of us. And this puzzle—the big picture of our lives—has a unique quality. Unlike other picture puzzles, the puzzle pieces of our lives can be assembled into an infinite number of different scenes, with no pieces left over and none omitted. This is good news! If we're weary of the old picture, there are always new possibilities.

SYMPTOM: *Anger*
Benefits:
1. *Shows that I value myself, as he did not*
2. *Expresses my sense of morality and human decency*
3. *Makes me feel big and powerful*
Backtalk:
1. *Rage actually subtracts from my life. If fills my bloodstream with stress chemicals and crowds out my positive feelings.*
2. *I'll be more likely to make good moral choices if my head and heart are clear.*
3. *Basing my power on victimhood keeps me in a victim position. Authentic power will come from an identity I choose for myself.*

Figure 5.2. Mary's New Deal

Above is another New Deal worksheet (figure 5.2), this one done by Mary, a woman who'd been sexually abused by her grandfather when she was a child.

EXPERIMENT V

⟳ The New Deal

Step One: Take out your lab book, date this entry, and write down a symptom you'd like to renegotiate. It could be an unhelpful belief (*the world is a completely dangerous place*), a negative thought (*I'm not getting better*), an unhealthy negative emotion (anxiety, bitterness, hopelessness), or a self-sabotaging behavior (avoidance, drinking too much, procrastination, and so on).

Step Two: Write beneath this symptom all the benefits it brings.

Step Three: Write down your backtalk to each of these benefits.

How did you do with talking back to the old deal and laying a foundation for a new one? If your backtalk won the dispute, this symptom is likely a candidate for the tools we'll describe next. If your backtalk sounded less than convincing, this might signal it's not yet time to strike a new deal related to this symptom. In the latter case it might be better to select another symptom to explore for hidden wisdom, set a price on, and consider for its own new deal.

Figure 5.3 is a flowchart to help you keep track of where you are in the process of deciding which symptoms you want to work to reduce or eliminate, and which you would prefer to leave in place for the time being.

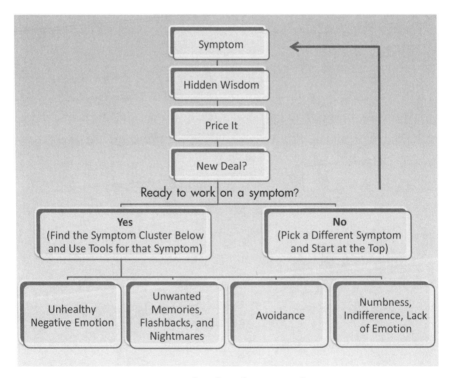

Figure 5.3. Flowchart for CBT Tool Use

The remaining sections in this chapter will present CBT tools specifically designed to address four categories of PTSD symptoms: unhealthy negative emotion; flashbacks, unwanted memories, and nightmares; avoidance; and indifference, numbness, and lack of motivation. Please note that tools presented in one section might also help with symptoms in another. These categories generally coexist alongside one another. Negative emotion, for instance, is an essential part of avoidance. Lack of motivation is a common reason we isolate ourselves from others. Mastering the tools in all six sections will give you a world-class toolbox with which to bring about any change you're ready to make in your life.

SYMPTOM CLUSTER: UNHEALTHY NEGATIVE EMOTION

In an early paper Albert Ellis wrote, "Much of what we call emotion is nothing more or less than a certain kind—a biased, prejudiced, or strongly evaluative kind—of thought. Negative human emotions, such as feelings of anger or depression, generally are caused by some form or variation of the sentence 'This is bad!'"[1]

When we become aware of an unhealthy negative emotion we can drill down to identify the negative thoughts that are producing it. Negative thoughts are triggered by something outside the self—something someone else says or does, for example. But as the Greek Stoics noted, outside events don't produce "commotions of the mind." It's what we *say* to ourselves about these outside events that causes emotional suffering in our lives.

For our purposes, a negative thought is a declarative sentence that creates negative emotion. Remember that such sentences, conscious or subconscious, have two characteristics that give them the power to create negative emotion. First, they are distorted. Because they embody distortions such as telescopy, mirroring, clairvoyance, truthiness, and judgment, they are not good maps of reality. Second, we believe these statements to be true. Let's look at the connections between common negative emotions and the thought patterns we can drill down to locate beneath them.

Emotion: Anger
Negative thoughts: *He should not have done that to me. He should rot in hell for all eternity. He sentenced me to a life of loneliness and misery.*

Can you identify some distortions in each of these negative thoughts? The first two embody judgment. The third, clairvoyance and, perhaps, microscopy (taking one moment in time as representative of all time going forward): *I'm suffering now and this now represents my whole life. There are no possibilities outside my present condition.*

Emotion: Hopelessness
Negative thoughts: *Nothing will change. I am powerless to create a different life. There's no chance things will ever work out.*

What are the distortions in these thoughts? We can find clairvoyance and microscopy in them. Perhaps also a distortion we call the secret judge. Hiding in the statement *Nothing will change* might well be the idea *But things* should *change!* Without the secret judge the thought *Nothing will change* might not create negative emotion. It might actually produce great positive emotion. People in heaven might have this thought and derive great happiness from it. But when a secret judge is sitting in such a statement it will always produce emotional distress.

Emotion: Worthlessness
Negative thoughts: *I'm damaged goods. Nobody likes me. I'll never get anything right.*

Can you identify the distortions in these thoughts? In fact each of them might contain all the distortions we've considered so far. Frequently our negative thoughts are distorted in multiple ways. They present themselves as the plain truth but are in fact very poor maps of reality. Identifying the distortions in each is an important step toward talking back to such thoughts. Each distortion is a chink in a negative thought's armor, a place in which it is vulnerable to the entry of reason and the scientific method. For easy reference, here is a list of common distortions that regularly crop up in our thinking:

Distorted Thinking

Clairvoyance: telling ourselves we know the future or can read others' minds

Truthiness: believing a gut feeling instead of the data

Judge/secret judge: usually a "should" statement—telling ourselves that we, others, or the world should or should not be a certain way

Microscopy: focusing so closely on one thing we miss the bigger picture

Telescopy: viewing some event from the distant past or future as the ever-present, defining feature of our lives

Mirroring: telling ourselves what happens in the world (or within others) is our fault, and that we are responsible for any bad thing that happens

Perfectionism: demanding that we or others always get things "just right"

Any of these basic distortions can take many forms. You can create names for your own. One patient developed her own version of microscopy, which she called "horrible-izing." It described her habit of calling any setback she encountered "horrible"—catastrophic, devastating, and insurmountable. She began referring to herself in such moments as her own Hannibal Lecter! Another patient created the distortion "martyrdom," which captured the personalization that occurred when she told herself things like *This always happens to me. I can never catch a break.*

The next two tools are powerful techniques we can use to begin re-scripting the distorted, "biased, prejudiced, strongly evaluative" thought processes that Albert Ellis insightfully observed produce unhealthy negative emotion in our lives.

Drill Down

Reducing or eliminating unhealthy negative emotion is a primary goal of psychotherapy. CBT helps reach this goal by focusing not on the emotion itself but on the underlying thought patterns that are creating such emotion. Once we identify this thinking we again refocus, not on the thought but on our belief in the thought. A distorted thought is powerless to cause suffering so long as we don't believe or *invest* in it. Our next tool helps identify negative thoughts. The following tool specifically addresses investment or belief.

EXPERIMENT VI

꙳ Drill Down

Step One: Take out your lab book, date this entry, and write down a negative feeling a New Deal has shown you're ready to reduce or eliminate. After the feeling write a number between 1 and 100 that reflects the intensity of that feeling right now.

Step Two: Ask yourself, What am I telling myself that is producing this feeling? Write down the negative thoughts that are producing this emotion, leaving a few lines between each statement. After each thought write a number between 1 and 100. This number reflects your degree of belief in that statement right now.

Step Three: Beneath each statement write the names of the distortions present in each thought.

Step Four: Explain aloud to yourself or to a lab partner of your choice how each thought is an example of each particular distortion. For example, considering the thought *I'm damaged goods* we could say aloud, "This thought contains microcopy because it focuses on hurt parts of myself and leaves out all the others. It has a secret judge who is saying I shouldn't have damaged parts. It might also contain clairvoyance, suggesting how I am right now is how I will be for all time." Saying your own words out loud is an important part of this experiment. Research suggests that our spoken words are more effective than silent self-talk. Don't be bashful! Speak up for yourself!

Step Five: Re-rate and write down the current intensity of the original feeling, and your current degree of belief in each statement.

Are you beginning to see the connection between your distorted thinking and the negative feelings it produces? Your thought patterns comprise your cognitive "fingerprint." Your physical fingerprints are somewhat like all other people's and somewhat different as well. So too is your cognitive fingerprint. As you recognize the ways in which you characteristically distort your thinking you will begin earlier on to recognize distorted thoughts. When judgment offers itself you can consider whether you want to entertain the judge at that time. Knowing the emotional price you'll pay for keeping such company you may decide you'd prefer a different companion.

After identifying their distortions did your belief in any of your negative thoughts change? Sometimes simply analyzing the structure of a distorted thought will reduce our belief in it. Writing down a thought or saying it aloud can have the same effect. If your belief in a thought went down, did the intensity of the negative emotion associated with it go down as well? This is what we would expect to see happen. When we reduce or eliminate our belief in a negative thought we reduce or eliminate the emotion it is producing. These thoughts are like props holding up the negative emotion. When we kick the props out, the emotion itself comes tumbling down.

Get Real

Let's assume you're still feeling more of some negative emotion than you'd like to feel. This is probably because you're still somewhat invested in, or believing, the negative thought that is driving this feeling. We'll now share a tool designed further to reduce or completely eliminate your belief in any negative thought that is upsetting you. Called "Get Real," this tool helps you discard old, distorted maps of your world for new, reality-based maps. As you recall, reality-based maps never create negative emotion. They instead help us get to places we want to go, which produces positive emotion, motivation, and the belief we can and do create the life we most want.

EXPERIMENT VII

⟋ Get Real

Step One: Take out your lab book, date this entry, and write down a negative thought from the Drill Down exercise you'd like to work on further. After it, write the number between 1 and 100 that reflects your degree of belief in the thought right now.

Step Two: Write down and explain aloud the distortions present in the thought.

Step Three: Ask yourself, How can I restate this sentence in a way that both eliminates its distortions and rings true to me? Write down then say aloud your new, undistorted thought. After it, write a number between 1 and 100 that reflects how much you believe it.

Step Four: Go back and re-rate your degree of belief in the original negative thought.

Figures 5.4–6 (pages 59–60) show some Get Real worksheets completed by our patients.

Notice that removing the distortions and restating things in a more realistic way tended to bring down the degree of belief in the negative thought. Sometimes this work completely eliminated belief in the old thought, sometimes not. Also patients sometimes completely believed the new thought, sometimes not. Generally speaking, the more we believe the new, reality-based thought, the less we'll believe the old, distorted thought. You will be the one to decide when this work is done. If reducing belief in a negative thought to single-digit levels reduces the negative emotion associated with it to an acceptable level, you might consider work on that thought to be complete. If you're still believing the old, distorted thought more than you'd care to, you can move on and try one of the tools we'll present next.

NEGATIVE THOUGHT: *I'll never feel happy again*

Percent Belief in the Negative Thought: *100%*

Distortions: *1. Microscopy*
2. Truthiness

New, Undistorted Thought:
While I'm very unhappy right now I can take steps to create moments of joy in my life. If I do so I'll get better at doing this more of the time.

Percent Belief in the New Thought: *95%*

Percent Belief in the Original Negative Thought: *10%*

Figure 5.4. Get Real sample 1

NEGATIVE THOUGHT: *Given my childhood I am just a defective human being*
Percent Belief in the Negative Thought: *95%*
Distortions: *1. Telescopy*
2. Microscopy
3. Secret Judge
4. Perfectionism
New, Undistorted Thought:
Terrible things happened to me, which affected me deeply; I also have certain positive qualities. In this way I'm like any other human being.
Percent Belief in the New Thought: *100%*
Percent Belief in the Original Negative Thought: *0%*

Figure 5.5. Get Real sample 2

NEGATIVE THOUGHT: *He's mad again and it's my fault*
Percent Belief in the Negative Thought: *100%*
Distortions: *1. Mirroring*
2. Secret Judge
New, Undistorted Thought:
He's angry because of what he's saying to me and to himself. His anger is about him, not about me.
Percent Belief in the New Thought: *85%*
Percent Belief in the Original Negative Thought: *20%*

Figure 5.6. Get Real sample 3

Kernel of Truth

One way negative thoughts keep their hooks in us is by containing a kernel of truth. A negative thought without any validity at all will probably just sound silly. Unless we've watched way too many science fiction films, the thought *I'm about to be abducted by squeaky green aliens who will take me to a far planet and extract my DNA* is unlikely to ring true. Whereas the thought *Somebody is out to get me* might ring very true if we've once been attacked and are involved in avoidance behavior that reminds our brain we're constantly in great peril.

Extracting the kernel of truth in a negative thought, recognizing it, and restating it in a new, undistorted way can sometimes bring great relief. It can satisfy that part of our brain that wants to alert us to something—potential danger, say—yet broker a new deal that allows us to leave behind the unhealthy negative emotion associated with this truth. Here's another experiment you can run on any negative thought, followed by examples of how patients have completed it.

EXPERIMENT VIII

⮿ Kernel of Truth

Step One: Take out your lab book, date this entry, and write down a negative thought you'd like to work on resolving. After it, write the number between 1 and 100 that reflects your degree of belief in the thought right now.

Step Two: List and say aloud the distortions present in the thought.

Step Three: Ask yourself, What kernel of truth exists in this statement? Write down and say aloud a new statement that both acknowledges this truth and is free of distortions. Write your degree of belief in this restatement.

Step Four: Go back and re-rate your degree of belief in the original negative thought.

Figures 5.7–9 (pages 62–63) are some examples of how patients identified their kernels of truth.

NEGATIVE THOUGHT: *My life is a complete waste*

Percent Belief in the Negative Thought: *95%*

Distortions: *1. Microscopy*
2. Secret Judge
3. Truthiness
4. Perfectionism

Kernel of Truth:
I have wasted much time and many
opportunities. I have much time left and new
opportunities await me. I can make of these
whatever I want.

Percent Belief in the Restatement: *95%*

Percent Belief in the Original Negative
Thought: *20%*

Figure 5.7. Kernel of Truth sample 1

NEGATIVE THOUGHT: *Nobody likes me*

Percent Belief in the Negative Thought: *80%*

Distortion: *Microscopy*

Kernel of Truth:
Some people certainly don't like me. Some people do.

Percent Belief in the Restatement : *100%*

Percent Belief in the Original Negative
Thought: *0%*

Figure 5.8. Kernel of Truth sample 2

NEGATIVE THOUGHT: I deserve all the bad things that happen to me

Percent Belief in the Thought: 100%

Distortions: 1. Mirroring
*   2. Truthiness*
*   3. Secret Judge*

Kernel of Truth:
I bear some responsibility for events in my life.
What I most deserve is happiness, respect, and the right to choose the life I now want.

Percent Belief in the Restatement: 95%

Percent Belief in the Original Negative Thought: 5%

Figure 5.9. Kernel of Truth sample 3

Did the Kernel of Truth process help you with a negative thought? If so, great! If not, great! Keeping this exercise in your toolbox for future use, let's move on to our next tool.

Play Doubles

In court sports such as tennis, two people sometimes team up on the same side of the net. Doing so increases their coverage of the court and raises the probability they'll successfully return an incoming volley. In the late nineteenth century the French social psychologist Emile Durkheim coined the term "collective consciousness" to describe the benefits of this phenomenon in the mental realm. Today we might call it "crowdsourcing a solution." By increasing the IQ points we bring to a challenge, we increase the probability we'll rise to meet it.

In our PTSD treatment groups a member will sometimes ask for help responding to a particularly challenging negative thought. When her own backtalk is not carrying the day, another group member's backtalk might get the job done. You don't need a PTSD group to partner with you in this way. Any caring friend or family member can join your team. For this approach really to offer the possibility of helping, two rules apply:

1. Your partner refrains from offering sympathy, advice, or reassurance.
2. Your partner simply supplies possible backtalk that might help reduce or eliminate your belief in a negative thought.

While these conditions sound straightforward they can be challenging for a loved one who cares about us and wants to help relieve our suffering. If our negative thought is *I'm just no damn good,* sympathetic responses such as "I'm sad hearing you say that" won't help. Neither will such nuggets of advice as "You just need to look at the bright side of things," or of reassurance, "Actually you're really great!" What will help us are new "I statements" that we can test drive in our own brains. Here is some backtalk one of our PTSD groups generated to help a member with the thought *I'm just no damn good:*

> *Certain things I'm no damn good at. Other things I do well enough. The same can be said of any human being.*
> *My own goodness, like other people's, has to do with my being, not my doing. I'm a good person who does both well and poorly at different things.*
> *This is what I've been told since childhood. It represents other people's opinions, not a statement of fact.*

The first two offerings didn't help this patient at all. The third statement rang completely true for this woman who had been plagued by this thought her entire life. Seeing through this "truth" about herself she started laughing out loud and feeling joyful for the first time in many years. It was wonderful to watch her take her first breaths of freedom from this belief she'd been living with since early childhood.

EXPERIMENT IX

◌ Play Doubles

Step One: Take out your lab book, date this entry, and write down a negative thought you'd like help with from someone else. After it, write the number between 1 and 100 that reflects your degree of belief in the thought right now.

Step Two: List and speak aloud the distortions present in the thought.

Step Three: Explain to a partner the rules of the game and invite him or her to help talk back to the thought. Frequently a partner will open a new line of thinking that you can then take up and improve. Some back and forth with a partner can help refine the backtalk to make it as powerful as possible.

Step Four: Write down, say aloud, and record your belief in the new, reality-based thought.

Step Five: Re-rate your degree of belief in the old, distorted thought.

Schedule It

Cognitive tools that address our beliefs and thought patterns comprise half the CBT toolkit. The other half is made up of behavioral tools—ways of changing up what we *do* during our day. The Schedule It tool combines these two approaches. It addresses chronic negative feeling states by setting aside a certain portion of each day in which to feel anxious, sad, hopeless, or angry. Fifteen to twenty minutes is a good amount of time. This tool is sometimes tremendously helpful in consolidating, reducing, or eliminating negative emotion. Perhaps when we give our brains free reign to do something—worry, say—the neuronal circuits associated with this state eventually burn themselves out like a lightbulb filament that gets too much current for too long.

Here are some guidelines for scheduling negative emotion:

1. Set a timer for a particular amount of time, ideally the same time each day.
2. Make sure you will not be interrupted or distracted during this time.
3. Create as much of the emotion you've scheduled as possible; try to get its intensity to 100 percent and keep it there the entire time.
4. When the timer goes off, set aside these thought patterns and the feelings they produce until the same time slot tomorrow. If they return during other times, remind your brain it will have the opportunity to take them up again soon.

We can also schedule problem solving in our lives so that it isn't all-consuming, interfering with our focus, happiness, and even sleep. In this instance write down in your lab book the problem at hand and set a timer. Now brainstorm and write down all the possible ways to address this problem. When the timer goes off, set aside such thinking until the same time the following day. If you've written down action steps, go ahead and take them, as this will be an important part of resolving and leaving behind problems in your life.

Consult the Data

A certain class of negative thoughts embody the distortion "truthiness"— our going with a "gut feeling" about something and ignoring the actual data. Patients tell us *I just* feel *worthless. I wouldn't have this feeling if it weren't so.* Truthiness takes a *feeling* that something is true as *proof* that it is true. *If I'm feeling unsafe I must be at risk. If I feel I have no future I must not have one.* As Stephen Colbert has noted, this distortion can get writ large on the international stage when a political leader "just knows" he or she is right about something, then acts on a gut feeling in the face of all evidence to the contrary.

Trauma can change our belief system in such a way that external events will trigger truthy thoughts that create emotional suffering. Neil suffered crushing financial losses in what turned out to be a massive Wall Street pyramid scheme. His belief that he was financially stable changed overnight. Neil was forced out of retirement and began being tormented by the thought *I'm running out of money,* which created a great deal of fear, hopelessness, and shame. By now you can probably see how this thought was a solution Neil's brain came up with to keep him more vigilant about his finances. But this approach was creating great suffering for Neil, and he wanted to find a better way forward in his new reality.

We asked Neil to consult the data and he began referring to his account statements whenever this thought arose. Much to his surprise, the numbers did not match up with this thought. Neil was on solid financial footing and steadily rebuilding the wealth that had been stolen from him. After regularly consulting the data, Neil's belief reset to what it had been before his financial crisis. If and when the thought *I'm running out of money* came up, it now seemed ridiculous to Neil. The data about his financial condition displaced his belief in this thought and Neil ceased being plagued by the fear and stress it had caused. If the thought ever did trouble him he simply referred to his account statements and immediately felt better.

Suzie's situation involved social capital, not money. Suzie had been cast out of her faith community when she came forward with information about the misconduct of its charismatic leader. This massive public shunning had a devastating impact on her. She began telling herself *Nobody likes me* and *I have no friends,* isolating herself and feeling tremendously worthless, lonely, and unloved.

We asked Suzie to consult the data so she created an Excel spreadsheet and did an exhaustive accounting of all the people in her life. The tally astonished her. While it was true that some people she'd considered friends no longer spoke to her, the data showed there were many more who were still friends or potential friends. Suzie decided to reach out to this new community and rather quickly found herself somewhat overwhelmed by the demands of her renewed social life. Her Excel data and the new brain data she created by changing her behavior and again connecting with people rendered thoughts such as *Nobody likes me* completely implausible.

EXPERIMENT X

⌒ Consult the Data

Step One: Take out your lab book, date this entry, and write down a negative thought you'd like help with. After it, write the number between 1 and 100 that reflects your degree of belief in the thought right now.

Step Two: List and speak aloud the distortions present in the thought.

Step Three: Consult the data. Collect actual, physical evidence for and against this thought.

Step Four: Compare the evidence for and against the thought.

Step Five: Re-rate your degree of belief in the negative thought.

Embrace

Martial arts such as aikido and t'ai chi are built around the principle of responding to an attack in an open, receptive, and relaxed way. Instead of opposing an attack, tensing up, or trying to avoid it, the student learns to prevail by connecting with the energy being presented and using it in whatever way she wants. It's wonderful to see this done masterfully. The scariest attacks turn into a kind of dance, with the student remaining calm, composed, and in quiet command each step of the way.

What Eastern martial arts teach on the physical realm is an approach we can take to our own negative thoughts. Instead of opposing distorted thinking we can choose to embrace it, to "go with" rather than against these cognitive attacks on our person. Let's look at how we might embrace some common negative thoughts and thus "win" our encounter with them.

Negative Thought: *I'm just not good enough.*
Embrace: *So true! And what a great thing this is. There is no area of life in which I can't step up my game and experience even greater accomplishment, success, and happiness.*

Negative thought: *I have no future.*
Embrace: *What a load off my mind! Now I can just relax and enjoy today. That's all I'll ever need or want to do.*

Negative thought: *People think I'm ridiculous.*
Embrace: *I do, too! My silliness is a gift to myself and others. I don't have to take myself seriously all the time. I can regularly channel my comic side and have fun.*

Negative thought: *I'm just a nobody.*
Embrace: *And loving it! I don't have to keep up pretenses. I have the freedom to choose moment to moment to be whomever I want. Sounds perfect!*

The key to using this tool is finding a way to accept and even embrace a negative thought such that it creates *positive* emotion, not the *negative* emotion the thought had previously produced. Embracing *I'm a worthless human being* by saying *That's true* and then collapsing into worthlessness, shame, and self-loathing won't help at all. We're looking for a response that will generate *positive* feelings. Here's an embrace one patient made to this very thought: *So true! The word "worth" is a human invention, activity in the frontal lobe of my brain. There is no way this word captures the real meaning or complexity of human life. I am who I am. And that's good enough for me.*

EXPERIMENT XI

Embrace

Step One: Take out your lab book, date this entry, and write down a negative thought you'd like help with. After it, write the number between 1 and 100 that reflects your degree of upset caused by this thought.

Step Two: List and speak aloud the distortions present in the thought.

Step Three: Embrace the thought. Say aloud how this thought expresses something awesome, valuable, and important about who you are.

Step Four: Re-rate your degree of upset associated with this thought.

SYMPTOM CLUSTER: UNWANTED MEMORIES, FLASHBACKS, AND NIGHTMARES

When trauma strikes our lives it can have ripple effects throughout space and time. A bad thing that happened to us "back there, back then" can keep reappearing in our present-day lives. As such it may be a most unwelcome visitor. Awake or asleep, by ourselves or with others, the experiences, emotions, and physical reactions we once had can again take center stage. When this happens we begin to lose contact with "here and now." Intrusive memories might appear like an unwanted movie playing out on the screen of our present-day lives. In the case of nightmares and what we call "flashbacks," these memories can completely crowd out our present-day reality, plunging us physically and mentally back into a terrifying and painful past. If we view these ripple effects as expressions of a disease process we may feel ashamed, resentful, and hopeless about ever being rid of them. Many doctors subscribe to this view and give patients pills that may or may not mitigate the suffering these symptoms cause. Whether such pills help or not they very often produce side effects that then become problems of their own.

We see these symptoms in a very different way—as the brain's best effort to date to keep us alive, protected, and whole. In other words, the brain is doing the best it can with the knowledge and skills it already has. We can work with these kinds of symptoms with all the tools we've presented. If the symptom is a recurrent flashback, for instance, we can find the flashback's hidden wisdom, price its benefits, and then take our brains to the bargaining table to negotiate a new deal. These would be important first steps to take to understand and appreciate our brain's rationale for producing such symptoms. The experiments below present additional tools specifically for this class of experiences.

Talk It Out

You might remember Abe, the combat veteran who would be disturbed when sitting alone in a beautiful setting by hearing the screams of his dying men. These flashbacks had continued for many years, leading to Abe's feeling that he always had to stay busy to keep these voices at bay. He never felt able to relax and enjoy himself doing things like fishing, which he'd loved as a boy. Abe's doctor told him that PTSD was incurable and that the only thing he could do was give Abe powerful drugs to lessen the effects of his symptoms. Abe was not satisfied with this answer and came to us for help.

We led Abe through the Hidden Wisdom and Price It tools. Abe became convinced he was ready for a new deal, but we had one final question for him:

"Abe, you were these young men's commanding officer. Their parents entrusted you with their safe return from war. But they returned home in pine boxes. So you've stood by these anguished spirits in their last moments for many years, as befits a commanding officer. Are you saying now you're going to walk away from these young men, to abandon your post at their sides? How could you justify such a thing? What would you say to their parents?"

Perhaps you can see how this question addressed Abe's hidden wisdom. His flashbacks were a direct expression of his good heart, his human sadness, his devotion to duty and commitment to his men. When we asked this Abe took a long breath then replied:

"Yes, I *am* ready to walk away. I'm retired now. I've done my duty—and then some. The war ended decades ago. It's time I declare peace in my own home."

We instructed Abe to go home and sit in the quiet place where these flashbacks always occurred. We had him write out and rehearse with us what he would say when they came around. That evening he had the opportunity to deliver his message, which went like this:

"I think I understand why we've been meeting. Perhaps these meetings once served a purpose for both of us. But I'm not going to do this anymore. This is no longer helping either of us. I'm going to move on and it's time you do the same. That's a direct order. I'm through with you. Go."

This was the beginning of the end of Abe's flashbacks. They became fewer and farther between and Abe did indeed declare peace in his home and on his farm. Three weeks after first talking it out with his dying men, Abe caught his first fish in forty years.

EXPERIMENT XII

ஒ Talk It Out

Step One: Take out your lab book, date this entry, and write down an intrusive symptom—flashback or dream—you'd like to talk it out with and resolve. Note how often the symptom is occurring.

Step Two: Write out and practice aloud what you want to say to this symptom the next time it occurs. Pay particular attention to addressing what emerges when uncovering the symptom's hidden wisdom. This will be essential for your statement to have real power.

Record your statement and listen to it. Does it sound like you mean it? If not, rehearse until you hear in your voice an unmistakable note of conviction.

Step Three: The next time the symptom appears, talk it out. Keep doing so each time this symptom presents itself.

Step Four: If the symptom recurs, track how often it does so compared to the rate at which it occurred before talking it out.

Return to the Scene

Flashbacks and trauma-related nightmares are rooted in a historical place and time—an accident or crime scene, battleground, or other setting. When events from that place and time have not found their right place in the big picture of our present-day lives they might keep coming around, asking to be given attention. Our efforts to keep them out create a civil war within ourselves. Different parts of our experience, past and present, vie with each other and neither can completely carry the day.

A way out of this standoff is voluntarily to return to the scene. Here our present-day selves walk back into that historical place and time and join forces with earlier parts of ourselves. By turning toward rather than away from these experiences we open up the possibility of integrating them into our lives, bringing them in from the cold, and finding a place for them at the table. Let's look at how one patient returned—and found all parts of himself peacefully at home at last.

While in middle school Paul had been sexually abused by an older stepbrother. Now in his midthirties, Paul had not seen his stepbrother for many years. Yet when having sex with his wife Paul had flashbacks of his abuse that frightened and angered him, and confused both him and his wife. Paul began to feel hopeless and bitter, telling himself he'd never be able to have an intimate encounter that did not include his stepbrother and memories of what he'd done.

We took Paul through the Hidden Wisdom and Price It processes and he convinced himself and us he was ready to leave these flashbacks behind. We explained the Return to the Scene tool and the rationale behind this approach to recovery. Paul bravely agreed to return and we set up an extended therapy session in which to do this. It began with Paul closing his eyes and getting physically comfortable in a big chair. We had Paul do the abdominal breathing outlined in Experiment II so that he could become as relaxed and open as possible.

We then had the adult Paul walk back into the setting in which he had been abused and describe it aloud in as much detail as possible. We asked about the sights, sounds, and smells in that place. Paul then met and hugged his younger self in that scene and they talked together about how happy they were to see each other. Younger Paul spoke about his fear, loneliness, shame, and confusion about what was happening to him. Present-day Paul wept and expressed his anger, sadness, and desire to protect and reassure his younger self. They then brought in their stepbrother and told him all the feelings that neither Paul had ever had the opportunity to express. Stepbrother sat silently and listened to everything each Paul had to say. Stepbrother then left the room and the two Pauls said goodbye—the older reassuring the younger that all would be well and the younger thanking the older for "coming back" after all these years.

After this heartfelt encounter Paul's flashbacks began to change. He said it was as though the bulb in a movie projector started to dim. The flashbacks continued for a while but each time they were a little fainter. At the same time Paul's present-day experience became brighter and brighter. He felt increasingly connected to his wife and able to focus on this connection while having sex with her. On his own Paul returned a few more times to hang out with his younger self. Months later Paul told us he had come to see his former flashbacks in a new light. They now seemed to be not about his stepbrother but about his relationship with his younger *self*. It was the younger Paul who had kept reaching out in this way, knowing how important it was for the boy and the man to connect. Once they reconnected Paul's entire emotional life and all the relationships in his life took on a new warmth, closeness, and satisfaction.

The Return tool can be used in many ways. We can, as adults, travel back in time to reconnect with any earlier version of ourselves. We can return to any nightmare and bring to it our daytime consciousness and the resources we have in our waking state. We can also edit our return in any way we'd like, bringing in any other people or resources we'd like at hand. We may rewrite the ending in any way we'd like. As did Paul, you might discover a meaning to the symptom or nightmare you would not have found if you hadn't returned—a buried treasure that will enrich your present-day life in ways you've never imagined possible.

EXPERIMENT XIII

〰 Return to the Scene

Step One: Take out your lab book, date this entry, and write down an intrusive symptom to work on resolving.

Step Two: Sit comfortably, close your eyes, and do a few minutes of abdominal breathing.

Step Three: Return to the scene and, with nobody else there, take it in through all your senses. Really immerse yourself there. As you do so you may enter a daydream state and be somewhat dissociated from your "here and now." This is fine. Your job now is to be, as your present-day self, "there and then."

Step Four: Bring in any and all parties you want there with you and say, shout, or scream anything at all you would want these parties to hear. You can also invite them to speak to you or to each other and listen to what they might have to say. It can be especially powerful to speak to the feelings in the air, both past and present.

Step Five: Do any editing you might want to do to this imaginal footage. If working with a nightmare you can "rewrite"—with paper and pencil—the dream in any direction you'd like it to go. Acting out your written script, speaking aloud your new parts, will light up those sections of your brain that pay particular attention to public pronouncements.

Step Six: Say your goodbyes and slowly, in your own time and way, return to here and now.

Step Seven: On the next page of your lab book keep track of changes that occur in the frequency or intensity of this symptom going forward.

Dream Decoder

Sometimes our nightmares contain none of the overt details of a trauma we've experienced. Perhaps our trauma is a motorcycle accident. Soon afterward we might begin having terrifying dreams of a wild animal breaking into our homes and attacking us or our children. What might be the meaning of such dreams?

The subconscious mind, ground from which our dreams emerge, is a poet, not an accountant. It is the storehouse for all our experiences as well as for what esteemed psychiatrist Carl Jung called the "collective subconscious"—content we share with all other members of our species and the archetypes we hold in common. In dreams our mind presents this material to us imagistically. One thing stands in for another. Space-time and real-imaginary are collapsed. Great grandmother walks in as a young girl. The black bear we saw in the woods as a child sits in dad's armchair smoking a pipe.

Friends at the C. G. Jung Institute in Zurich shared with us a tool that has helped our patients "unpack" difficult recurrent dreams. The Dream Decoder tool works backward from the dream itself to what the dream might be pointing to in its imagistic way. To make this come alive we'll show how it helped decode one patient's recurring nightmare.

Arin was a very bright, creative young woman who normally

enjoyed her dreams. She was a vivid dreamer and had many exotic adventures while asleep—piloting flying carpets over world capitals, being reborn as a Hindu deity, winning gold medals in Olympic diving. One dream, which she did not enjoy at all, kept recurring. Unlike Arin's other dreams, this one was stark, unvarying, and disturbingly menacing. We had Arin begin to decode her dream by first writing it out:

> *No one appears in the dream. There is only a fully cooked Thanksgiving turkey set on a silver platter. And the sound of a drum, like a Native American drum, being played slowly and implacably in the background. I become more and more terrified, and startle wake in a cold sweat.*

Arin could not make heads or tails of this dream. It seemed surreal—like a Salvador Dali painting. At the same time it carried a feeling of dread more intense than anything she'd ever experienced, either awake or asleep. Once she'd written it out we had Arin highlight words on the page that seemed to have particular weight or pull on her psyche.

Here is her highlighting:

> *No one appears in the dream. There is only a fully cooked Thanksgiving turkey on a silver platter. And the sound of a drum, like a Native American drum, being played slowly and implacably in the background. I become more and more terrified, and startle wake in a cold sweat.*

We next had Arin write out the highlighted words and free associate to each of them. Free association is a tool developed by Sigmund Freud, the Austrian neurologist known as the "father of psychoanalysis." When we free associate we say aloud or write down words that spontaneously come to mind when we hear a word. These associations are "free" of any logical or conscious effort, emerging directly from our subconscious mind. Here's what Arin wrote:

Arin's Free Association

Word(s)	Free Association
No one	Death, loneliness, despair
Thanksgiving	Family, togetherness, gratitude
Silver platter	Life, all good things, privilege, ease
Sound of Drum	Heartbeat, ceremony, doom
Native American	Natural, first, wise
Implacably	Inevitable, futile to resist, stuck

Then from the list of highlighted words Arin again highlighted those that seemed to have the most emotional pull on her psyche:

Death, loneliness, despair

Family togetherness, gratitude

Life, all good things, privilege, ease

Heartbeat, ceremony, doom

Natural, first, wise

Inevitable, futile to resist, stuck

Finally we had Arin replace the original words in her dream with these last highlighted words to see what the dream might now be saying to her:

Arin's Highlighted Free Association Words

Original Word(s)	Free Associated Word(s)
No one	Death
Thanksgiving	Family togetherness
Silver platter	Privilege
Sound of drum	Heartbeat
Native American	Wise
Implacably	Futile to resist

Here is how her newly decoded dream looked:

Death appears. Family togetherness, our great privilege. Beating hearts. Wisdom: it is futile to resist.

Reading this version of her dream Arin began to weep. She'd recently lost her grandmother, to whom she'd been very close. It was her first experience of death and it was challenging all Arin's beliefs about herself and her world. Unable to come to terms with her feelings about this loss and the questions that it raised, Arin had swept them all under the carpet. Yet her subconscious mind knew how important it was to address these essential human themes, and so kept presenting them to her in the form of this recurring dream. Arin's decoded dream contained all these elements, ending with the deep wisdom of accepting love and loss and her particular place in the great cycle of living and dying. Once Arin saw what her own subconscious mind was urging upon her she courageously took up these themes in therapy and never again had this nightmare.

EXPERIMENT XIV

Dream Decoder

Step One: Write out in your lab book a dream you'd like to decode.

Step Two: Circle or highlight words in the dream that have particular pull on your psyche.

Step Three: Write these words in a column and your free associations to each.

Step Four: Highlight words in this second free association list that have particular weight.

Step Five: Replace the original words in your dream with words from this last list. See now what your dream might be saying to you.

SYMPTOM CLUSTER: AVOIDANCE

Bad things tend to draw more mental current than good things. Nature selects for this "negativity bias" because failing to attend to negative stimuli is potentially far more damaging than failure to attend to positive stimuli. If our forebears ignored signs of a saber-toothed tiger nearby while enjoying the call of a songbird, this choice might well decrease the probability those forebears would pass their genes on to the next generation! We can see expressions of this bias throughout our culture. "If it bleeds, it leads" has long been the newspaper editor's mantra when presenting the day's events. Best-selling books and movies oftentimes feature one or many very bad things indeed. Research has shown "attack ads" against a political opponent are a more successful strategy than ads that present a candidate's own positive qualities.

Following trauma we might experience this bias in our thoughts, feelings, and behaviors. If a toddler grabs a hot woodstove she will very likely avoid doing so a second time. Such avoidance has obvious benefits to her, representing her brain's best effort to date to help her avoid pain and remain well and whole. But this healthy inclination to avoid something bad might begin to draw too much mental bandwidth, to *overcorrect* her behavior. If she refuses to go into any room with a woodstove or demands that the word "woodstove" never be uttered in her presence, we can see that her solution to one problem has now become a problem of its own. When avoiding bad things becomes the central focus of our lives it becomes, paradoxically, yet another bad thing.

Saleena, for example, had been very close to her mother for the first five years of her life. Her mother was kind, attentive, and respectful of Saleena, and their home life in their rural community was a kind of Garden of Eden. This happy state of affairs changed dramatically on Saleena's first day of school at the village's one-room schoolhouse. The teacher was overwhelmed with keeping order and attempting to teach students ranging in age from five to twelve. As a result he developed a harsh and aggressive style of crowd control that involved threatening students with physical punishment for minor infractions of rules that Saleena could not quite understand. Saleena was terrified. She sat trembling in her place that first day, afraid to ask to use the bathroom until finally she wet herself. The teacher became enraged at Saleena for this "misconduct," and brought her to the front of the room and shamed her in front of the entire class.

Something broke inside Saleena that day, then reset in a direction that would cause her great suffering in the years ahead. Pleasing others and being perceived as "a good girl" became overriding concerns in her relationships. Saleena was frequently rewarded for behaviors in this direction. No one, not even Saleena, understood that her growing up had been hijacked by her trauma. Instead of developing into a young woman who knew and confidently presented herself to the world, she spent her days and nights overcorrecting, carefully avoiding any presentation of self that might produce conflict, condemnation, and the terrible shame that had ripped through the fabric of her young body, heart, and mind. Tiptoeing around her life in this way Saleena became increasingly depressed, frightened, and lonely.

Avoidance is a two-edged sword: one edge promotes life, the other takes life. The exposure tools we'll now present address this latter edge—"overcorrections" of behavior that create new problems of their own. The first edge generally takes care of itself. Few of us would repeatedly touch a hot stove, seek again to be swindled, or attempt repeatedly to contract a life-threatening illness. The second edge is trickier. We may lull ourselves into overcorrection without even noticing we're doing so. Then one day we may wake up to the fact that we're paying a very high price to avoid certain feelings, memories, situations, or activities. At this point we might reach for one of the exposure tools presented below.

"Exposure" is a CBT term for turning toward, instead of away from, fear triggers. A powerful tool, exposure carries a price tag: in the short term it *increases* our fear as we begin to take into our bodies and minds something we've trained ourselves to avoid. If there were another way to crush fear we would certainly prefer it! When we are suffering, opting to sign up for even *more* suffering seems like a patently bad idea. It's similar to the position of a person with a dislocated shoulder. In great pain, we want to feel better and protect ourselves by immobilizing the joint. Now a paramedic arrives and tells us she can relieve our suffering and put our shoulder back in place—by *pulling* on it. What are we going to do? We'll need strong motivation for wellness to be willing to stop protecting ourselves and open up the possibility of true healing.

Let's assume you've already identified the hidden wisdom of an avoidance behavior, priced it, and reached the conclusion that you're now ready to pay the price for healing. As in the case of a dislocated shoulder, you're prepared to let go of immobility in order to embrace a new approach to finding security and peace of body and mind. Any one of the tools you've learned thus far might be a good candidate to help you reach this new goal. The tools below are specifically designed to diminish or extinguish avoidance behaviors that have outworn their usefulness in our lives.

Facing the Dragon

"How should we be able to forget those ancient myths that are at the beginning of all peoples, the myths about dragons that at the last moment turn into princesses," wrote the poet Rainer Maria Rilke in his classic *Letters to a Young Poet.* "Perhaps all the dragons of our lives are princesses who are only waiting to see us act, just once, with beauty and courage."

Rilke speaks to two deep truths: By turning away from something fearful we make it even more fearful, and very often what we shy away from we secretly love. Our aversion to that thing is but an immature form of our attraction to it. Let's look a bit more at each of these points.

Let's say you grow up in a village located walking distance from the sea. Two paths, each quite like the other, connect the village to the beach. From an early age you are told it is very important always to take one path and to avoid the other. All your friends and neighbors follow this dictum. But one day curiosity wins out and you decide to take the other path. What will happen as you start down this new way?

Very likely you will begin to feel anxious, perhaps increasingly so as you lose sight of the village and all familiar waypoints. Why? This new path is, after all, essentially just like the old path. One reason you'll be apprehensive is that you've trained yourself to perceive this new path in a certain way. By avoiding it so regularly and for so long you've given your brain the message this path is indeed dangerous. Your brain has tabulated this data and noticed two things: you've avoided this path and you've safely walked to the beach each time. Each time you walked the old path you made the connection between it and safety a little bit stronger, a little more obviously "so."

So! A principal way we create fear is by avoiding the thing that instills fear. Each time we do so we activate the same neuronal circuitry in our brains. Over time those circuits begin to fire all on their own. Just as we might automatically fasten our seat belt when getting into a car we'll automatically run these other, rather less evidence-based security operations in our lives. We no longer "do" these things. It's more that they "do" us.

However Rilke wrote not only of fear, but also of love. This second point is also important. Again and again we've seen patients who'd developed elaborate security operations to avoid something fall in love with that very thing once they stopped turning away *from* and began turning *toward* it. Turning toward regularly becomes the doorway to profoundly new and rewarding vistas. Let's look at how this happened in Saleena's life.

Once Saleena saw how the terrible events of her first day of school had hijacked her personal growth and development, she resolved to begin turning toward not away from interactions with others that held the potential for disagreement, conflict, and judgment. We taught her how, respectfully, to speak her own heart and mind, especially when these seemed to run counter to those of people around her. At first it was terrifying for Saleena to take this new path forward. She had trained herself long and well in the opposite direction and acting against this training seemed extremely risky. She feared people would reject and condemn her and she would again be standing up shamefully in front of her whole world. We supported Saleena by teaching her assertiveness skills and helping her practice these in the safety of our offices until she felt ready to "go live" and speak up for herself in the larger world.

When she did this something previously unimaginable happened. As Saleena began expressing herself in more authentic ways she found out that not only did she *love* doing this, many *others* loved it as well. For the first time since the age of five Saleena brought her excellent heart and mind out of the shadows and let them shine. She herself felt hugely relieved and once again excited about herself and her life. Others told her they noticed a profound shift in Saleena that they too very much liked. Saleena now felt real to them in a way she never quite had in the past. This real woman was a lot more fun to be around and people began opening up to her in new and authentic ways.

When we were practicing with Saleena in our offices we were doing what is called *in vitro* work on her fear. *In vitro* is Latin for "within glass" and describes experiments done in a test tube, laboratory, or other artificial environment. This is often a good first step toward facing our fears. If we have public speaking anxiety we might first *imagine* ourselves up in front of a group giving a speech. It is likely that the same thoughts and feelings will come up in this imaginal setting as would arise in real life. Unlike in real life, when in vitro we can hit the pause or rewind button, analyzing and troubleshooting what is happening within our hearts and minds.

Once we've gotten more comfortable in this artificial environment we can take the final step of going *in vivo*—Latin for "within life." Transforming our lives, finally crushing our fear and stepping into happiness and success, always requires that we go in vivo. After much practice the tennis player must show up at the match. After intensive training on a rope two feet off the ground the high-wire artist must step out far above the heads of the crowd. Only in doing so can we prove to ourselves and to others who it is we've become.

Saleena went in vivo by taking the skills she'd learned in our offices into her real-life interactions with family and friends. Even more than the practice she'd done in our offices it was these real-world interactions and the data they produced that gave Saleena's brain the information it needed to reset back to its pre-trauma state.

EXPERIMENT XV

Face the Dragon, In Vitro

Step One: Take out your lab book, date this entry, and write down something you've been turning away from that you're ready now to give your attention. Write a number from 1 to 100 that reflects how afraid you are of that thing right now.

Step Two: Sit comfortably, close your eyes, and do a few minutes of abdominal breathing.

Step Three: Imagine yourself turning toward this thing you've been avoiding. Really immerse yourself in the details of this scene. Notice what you're saying to yourself and others, the emotions you're feeling, and your physical sensations.

Step Four: Keep turning toward until either your fear goes down or away, or a timer you've set for this experiment rings.

Step Five: Return to the here and now and re-rate how scary this thing feels to you now. Also write down and measure any positive emotions such as curiosity, confidence, or motivation that emerge from this experiment.

Step Six: Repeat this experiment as many times as you'd like to further drive down your fear.

EXPERIMENT XVI

Face the Dragon, In Vivo

Step One: Take out your lab book, date this entry, and write down something you've been turning away from that you'd like now to address. Write a number from 1 to 100 that expresses how afraid you feel of that thing right now.

Step Two: Go out into the world and turn toward that thing. Play doubles if you'd like (and if having a friend along would be appropriate).

Step Three: Keep turning toward until either your fear goes down or away, or a timer you've set rings.

Step Four: Re-rate how scary this thing is to you now. Write down and measure any positive emotions such as curiosity, confidence, or motivation that emerge from this experiment.

Step Five: Repeat this experiment as many times as you'd like to further drive down your fear.

A last note on in vivo exposure: it is important once we start such work that we follow through with it. Beginning at last to walk toward the dragon, then changing our minds and running away will only remind our brains of the great danger we're in and make it more difficult ever again to approach that beast. Only when we're absolutely committed to walking right into the dragon's lair, sitting down and getting to know our dragon on a first-name basis, will in vivo exposure be indicated.

Put It into the Dance

Exposure exercises can take myriad forms. Turning toward instead of avoiding or covering over difficult situations, feelings, and experiences is frequently the active ingredient in trauma recovery. Finding creative, life-giving ways to turn toward can be a powerful experience for all concerned. One patient, a visual artist, calls this her Rumpelstiltskin work: saving her life by "weaving straw into gold."

Another kind of artist, a professional dancer named Juan, lost his life partner to AIDS. Juan was devastated by this death. He plunged into a deep depression and felt a powerful urge to turn away from life itself. Without his soulmate and love of his life, Juan saw no point in living. Sensing Juan's anguish one of his elderly teachers took him aside and offered to hear anything Juan might want to share. Juan opened up, weeping and pouring out all his grief, loneliness, anger, and despair. His mentor sat quietly, nodding and listening to it all. When Juan grew quiet the old man took Juan's hand, looked him in the eye, and said softly, "Put it into the dance."

"I did," Juan told us, "and it saved my life." It also greatly deepened his understanding and expression of his art. As Juan's heart reopened he began feeling the music his art physically expressed in an entirely new way. His students, audience, and critics noticed this shift and more and more people sought out his work. Embracing instead of turning away from the loss of his partner paradoxically brought tremendous new relationship into Juan's life. It also put a new frame around this loss. Memories of his partner now produced *healthy* negative emotions such as sadness, and healthy positive emotions such as gratitude and appreciation. Juan began accepting and once again loving the big picture of his life past, present, and future.

Mary, the woman who as a girl was abused by her grandfather, was a painter. For years she had avoided going into her studio. A part of her knew that to be happy she needed to paint. Another part kept turning away from the openheartedness such work would require. Mary was tremendously angry about what had happened to her and frequently felt worthless as well. Opening herself to experiencing more of these feelings felt like a very bad idea. Her worthlessness had seeped into her artist soul as well. She continually asked herself, *What if I start painting again and it's no good?*

When we met Mary her best effort to date was sitting on the

proverbial fence. She did not completely relinquish her sense of herself as an artist but distracted herself from painting by telling herself she had "things to do first"—household chores, paying bills, cleaning out her garage, and so on. Neither did she completely turn away from feelings of anger and hopelessness, nor turn entirely toward them. So too she held on to her husband—at arm's length. Months, then years, passed and Mary became increasingly unhappy, hopeless, and isolated from others and from her true self.

After hearing Mary's story we helped her see how avoidance was keeping her stuck emotionally, relationally, and artistically. She used Hidden Wisdom and Price It and bravely decided to turn toward all these fronts in one fell swoop. She went into her studio at last and came back two weeks later with a large rolled canvas under her arm. We helped her unroll it and stood back to absorb it. What we saw took our breath away and brought tears to our eyes. Mary's entire past, present, and future lay before us in all its heartbreaking form, feeling, and complexity. Mary took us through all the aspects of her creation, explaining the connections between its parts and the emotion associated with each.

Mary had created a masterpiece. For the first time she'd pulled together her entire life, spinning it into gold. The act of producing this work was itself an important part of the picture; she had turned her struggle into performance art. As we processed this with her we saw two more important aspects of what lay before us: First, this performance could continue for the rest of her life—and Mary's happiness might well depend on it doing so. Second, for this Christian artist, this performance masterpiece had spiritual connotations. Mary believed that human life was God's masterpiece. She began to consider including herself in this view. Instead of seeing herself as worthless or damaged goods, her work opened the door to experiencing herself and the big picture of her particular life as one of God's great works.

We've been tremendously inspired by the work of Juan, Mary, and many others. Writers have produced wonderful writing. Photographers have made heartbreaking images. Singers have written songs that touch the hearts of those who hear them. These creations have regularly been the turning point in these people's recovery from trauma. These brave men and women decided to spin their personal straw into gold. In doing so they moved on from being passive victims of their experiences to being active creators of new life. In this regard they are godlike indeed. We are humbled before such work the way we are humbled by crimson sunsets, starry nights, and other treasures that come to us from the very heart of the universe.

EXPERIMENT XVII

🐿 Into Your Dance

Step One: Take out your lab book, date this entry, and write down some feeling, memory, or situation you've been turning away from that you'd like now to turn toward and address. Write a number between 1 and 100 that expresses how afraid you feel of that thing right now.

Step Two: Brainstorm ways of spinning this straw into gold. If you have a knack for words, you might write a poem or story. If music is close to your heart you could compose a song. Dance or other performance, painting, weaving, woodworking, or virtually any art form can also provide a venue in which to "spin."

Step Three: Start spinning your magical creation!

Step Four: Re-rate your fear of this symptom.

SYMPTOM CLUSTER: NUMBNESS, INDIFFERENCE, LACK OF MOTIVATION

One "best effort" the brain might make in response to trauma is turning down or turning off emotions. Unfeeling may appear preferable to feeling great fear, anger, worthlessness, or despair. Our brains might even consider numbness to be lifesaving. In a numbed-out condition we can continue to live our lives and do the things that must be done to survive. This strategy is similar to our brain's decision in a physical crisis. While trying to escape a life threat it might be wise not to feel physical damage taking place. This might have been the decision Rick's brain made when he was shot in combat yet felt no pain until he was out of harm's way. Physical and emotional numbness might be an excellent short-term strategy.

Indifference and a lack of motivation might likewise contain tremendous hidden wisdom. Not caring about people and things protects us from hurt and disappointment. If we've experienced others as uncaring or overtly hostile, or experienced life as consistently withholding good things from us, indifference makes a deep kind of sense. Likewise if our efforts have consistently not produced the desired outcomes, conserving energy by no longer trying seems a reasonable response. Behavioral researchers have induced "learned helplessness" in lab animals by consistently thwarting their efforts to influence their environment in positive ways. At the end of these experiments such animals curl up in a corner of their cages and stop making any effort whatsoever. Their brains seem to have priced it and decided to conserve any remaining energy for another day.

However successful they are in the short term, these distancing strategies come with a price tag. When our brains turn down or off their emotional centers, positive feelings also get dimmed or eliminated. At this time in our evolution we don't have the ability to block one class of feelings and remain truly open to some other class. If we walk the world with our ears stopped up to reduce the chances of hearing painful noises and harsh words, it's unlikely we'll hear birdsong, music, or words of love. Protective emotional numbing will necessarily turn down or off positive emotions such as joy, love, optimism, curiosity, and motivation.

We'll assume you've done the usual Hidden Wisdom and Price It experiments on numbing, indifference, or lack of motivation and you're ready to start feeling again. Feeling *everything*, as that's the only deal on the table. Good for you! While numbing may appear passive it actually takes tremendous physical and mental energy. By reopening to all the jeweled movements of your heart/mind, this energy will again be freed to put into creating more and more of the life you most want to live. As you go down this new road you will feel all manner of emotion, positive and negative. You can work with unhealthy negative emotion using any of the tools presented earlier in this chapter. Positive emotions—joy, optimism, self-worth—might feel somewhat strange at first. Or they might reappear like childhood friends we've not seen for many, many years.

Book of Life

When we are feeling numb or indifferent about our own lives we might still have the capacity to feel emotion on behalf of others. The Book of Life tool piggybacks on this natural empathy and puts it to work on feeling healthy negative and positive emotion toward ourselves.

Aya, her family, and their entire community had endured great trauma and dislocation in the course of her country's civil war. As any semblance of a normal childhood was repeatedly taken from her, Aya found herself increasingly apathetic about her fate. Terrible events continued around her but Aya seemed to have located an island of indifference in their midst. Aya eventually emigrated to another country and established an adult life there. But her old habits of heart and mind stayed in place. Now safe, married, and a mom, Aya began feeling uncomfortable with her indifference toward even her two wonderful children. She turned to us for help.

We had Aya write down the story of her life—in the third person. She substituted another name for her own and wrote out all that had happened to this "other girl" as she was growing up. This exercise helped Aya understand more about herself and the connections between major life events than she had seen while looking at her experience through her own eyes. She also began to experience some feelings for this "other" little girl, though the feelings seemed muted and far away.

Next we had Aya locate a dear friend who agreed to read the entire story back to Aya in a single sitting. Early on in this reading her friend's voice broke and she began to weep as she read the terrible things Aya had experienced. Hearing the sadness, love, and anger in her friend's voice a kind of dam broke inside Aya. Now all the repressed fear, anger, and sadness that had been locked inside her body and mind began to erupt. Her friend put down the story and the two women embraced each other for a long time, weeping tears of rage and grief and also voicing in a way they never had the love and gratitude they felt for each other.

As Aya's heart reopened she was able to envision a future she had not seen since she was very young. It was a future in which she might experience great joy, pleasure, hope, and connection with others. She now faced the hard work of creating this future from moment to moment in her present-day life. It was wonderful to watch Aya step up to this work with ever increasing determination, confidence, and joy.

EXPERIMENT XVIII

✑ Book of Life

Step One: Take out your lab book and date this entry. In your book or in a separate document write your life story out in the third person, using a name other than your own. It may help to break it out into chapters that are chunks of time; for example, "Birth to Five Years," "Ages Five to Ten," and so on. Focus on just the facts told in as objective a way as possible.

Step Two: Find an undisturbed time and place to read this story aloud to yourself. This time notice what emotions come up for you as you read. If a particular feeling emerges, stop reading and focus on your emotional experience. Enter into it as deeply as you wish for as long as you wish, locate it in your body, then continue reading aloud.

Step Three: Find a dear friend who will read the story aloud to you. Tell the friend to read slowly and deliberately, adding nothing to the story nor leaving anything out. Note in particular the tone of your friend's voice and any emotion he or she may be feeling.

Step Four: As feelings arise you may raise your hand, signaling for your friend to pause. Explore these feelings as deeply as you wish, within yourself or aloud with your friend.

Act As If It's So

Remember Cynthia, the woman who was mugged and who subsequently would scuttle furtively about her city at night? When Cynthia experimented with walking confidently down the center of "her" sidewalk, head erect, eyes focused a block ahead, two things happened. First, she began *feeling* more confident and self-possessed: her emotional brain reset, following her behavior. Second, *others* began responding differently to Cynthia. Recognizing the command Cynthia was bringing to their passing, people began deferring to *her*. These two changes played on each other, amplifying the effects of both.

When we want to enhance some positive feeling state we can follow Cynthia's magnificent lead. If we want to feel more confident we can begin acting as would a confident person, *before*—and this is important!—we feel this confidence ourselves. This "As If" behavior will precede the emotion itself. We'll need to get in the rhythm of the thing to have it begin to have its effect. We'll also need to have our environment close the feedback loop and provide us new data about ourselves, others, and the world. Only then will we be candidates for our brains making the emotional shift we're seeking.

Acting as if something is already so can be used to create and amplify any positive feeling. How might a happy person act? How might she dress, do her hair, walk? Where might she go? How would a guy people love to be around behave? When he walks into a room, what will he do with his face, eyes, and body language? What will a person with a bright future do when out in public, talking on the phone, meeting someone for the first time? The possibilities are endless.

A patient who is an actress found this tool extremely helpful. She was already very good at "getting into character" before walking out onto the stage. She decided to view her whole life as a stage and spent more and more time "in the character" she wished to be. Eventually she realized her words and actions were no longer an act. She'd now *become* that person and, as happened for Cynthia, her stage's *mise en scène* reset to match its new character actress.

EXPERIMENT XIX

℞ Act As If

Step One: Take out your lab book and date this entry. Write the name of a positive emotion you'd like to enact. Write a number between 0 and 100 that indicates how intensely you feel this emotion at this time.

Step Two: Write down all the behaviors you imagine of a person who is feeling 100 percent of this emotion.

Step Three: Alone and on your own, practice each of these behaviors. Don't worry about feeling phony or fraudulent. Of course you're a fraud . . . for now! Just be as convincing a fraud as you can be.

Step Four: Go live! If you're working on joy you might walk down your street whistling, smelling roses, petting dogs, and hailing neighbors and friends.

Step Five: Go home and re-rate your degree of that positive feeling.

Motivator

Many of us struggle to feel motivation, the "fuel" for accomplishing things and changing the structure of our lives. Trauma can particularly devastate motivation. As we've repeatedly seen, bad things that happen can make doing less and less seem like a better and better idea. Important first steps toward addressing this stagnant state of affairs would be the Hidden Wisdom and Price It tools. At the end of the day, remaining unmotivated might be our best choice for the future. If not, here's good news: we can actually *create* motivation to do things we've been waiting around to do until we feel motivated. Our Motivator tool will show you how.

Dopamine has long been recognized as one of the principal reward chemicals in our brains. When dopamine is released we feel good. Nature has designed our brains to reward us for doing things that increase our chance of passing our genes along to the next generation. Eating and making love are two obvious examples. Countless other activities also get rewarded in this way. In fact any goal-directed activity that results in reaching a goal triggers a dopamine release in our brains. Now researchers are beginning to understand that dopamine is also a "motivation molecule." When dopamine receptors light up in our brains we feel an increased desire to continue or repeat the activity that produced this effect. You can probably see why this would be so. We're hardwired to feel good. So doing something that produces good feelings will seem like a better and better idea.

The error we tend to make is waiting to do something *until* we feel motivated to do it. Do you see the problem here? This is like waiting to go on a wonderful vacation until we are already at our destination. This could be a very long wait indeed! But if we are willing to *start moving* in the vacation direction—making reservations, buying tickets, and so on—the probability that we will in fact enjoy that vacation becomes more likely. Waiting withholds dopamine, moving toward delivers it. Each little success we have along the way becomes its own dopamine delivery mechanism. Our excitement builds and with it our desire to see things through and reach our final goal.

Tom was a perfect example. After experiencing a series of family tragedies he dropped out of college and retreated more and more into himself. He stopped returning phone calls and going out with friends, and did the bare minimum required to survive financially. When he came to us Tom was in his late twenties, suicidally depressed, and deeply unmotivated even to get out of bed in the morning. His apartment was an external expression of his internal state. His bed was always unmade, dirty laundry piled up in a corner of his bedroom, unwashed dishes were stacked high in the kitchen. Tom was frightened by the internal and external condition of his life. He told us he wanted our help feeling motivated to live again. We told Tom we could help him if he'd be willing to make and stick to a simple behavioral plan. Tom agreed.

Week one of Tom's plan consisted of two items: setting an alarm, and getting up when the alarm went off and making his bed. Ready for a new deal, Tom did both of these items on day one. Then something surprising happened. Having gotten up and made his bed Tom felt somewhat better than he had for two years. He decided to go into the kitchen and do some dishes. And so his week went. When he came back seven days later, Tom told us his apartment looked like that of, in his words, "an adult, not a sullen teenager." Tom's depression scores had plummeted, his suicidality was gone, and his motivation to keep his feet on his new path had skyrocketed. Twelve months later Tom was finishing college, had a 4.0 GPA, and was applying to graduate school in a field he'd decided would be an interesting and rewarding life path.

What happened? At a molecular level Tom began dosing himself with dopamine. Starved for this feel-good neurotransmitter, Tom's brain greedily lapped it up and immediately put it to good use. Setting an alarm and getting out of and making his bed both rewarded his brain and created in it a craving for additional reward. Tom's behavior was his dopamine-delivery mechanism and motivator to continue taking daily steps toward creating a new life.

EXPERIMENT XX

ꙮ Motivator

> **Step One:** Take out your lab book and date this entry. Write down some behavior you'd like to increase your motivation to do. Write a number between 0 and 100 that indicates how motivated you feel to do this thing right now.

Step Two: Do that thing! Generally fifteen to twenty minutes is a sufficient amount of time. If you want to continue for a longer period, feel free to do so.

Step Three: Re-rate how motivated you now are to continue this activity or repeat it at some later time.

Opening the Flower of Awareness

Microscopy, the cognitive distortion that ratchets attention down on a single aspect of life, can overtake our entire perceptual field. Combined with negativity bias, microscopy can become an entire lifestyle. Day and night we then walk about consumed by our negative thought patterns and the emotional, physical, and relational worlds they create. Living in such a bleak place we might well check out emotionally, if only to be able to keep placing one foot in front of the other. Earlier in this chapter we looked at good reasons to do exactly this.

If a numbed-out existence ceases being our best road forward, any of the tools presented so far might help us find new footing. In addition to these cognitive and behavioral approaches there is a mindfulness-based approach some of our patients have found extremely useful. It has helped some begin to feel emotion again and helped others refocus from a single intense negative feeling to a wider range of both positive and negative emotions. Opening the Flower of Awareness is both simpler and oftentimes more challenging than our other tools. The following story illustrates how it can work.

Sara suddenly contracted a rare, life-threatening infection that required her to shutter her professional photography business and spend three months in a hospital. During this time she lost her right arm from the elbow down and her husband of twenty years announced he was leaving her. Her insurance company said it would not cover the bulk of her medical fees, leaving her with almost $200,000 of medical debt. Though Sara eventually recovered her health and was discharged from the hospital, her life lay in ruins. Her beautiful home was sold and with the small alimony available to her, she moved with her cat into a two-bedroom apartment.

Shortly after these events took place we met Sara. She worked hard with our cognitive and behavioral tools and made improvements to her mood, particularly in regard to her feelings of hopelessness about the future, shame about being "a one-armed bandit," and fear of being unable to support herself in her new life. One symptom did not budge: anger. Sara continued to be enraged at the disease that disfigured and almost killed her, at her husband for leaving her, and at the insurance company for its "bait and switch" marketing. Sara examined what this anger was costing her and realized rage represented a "poor deal." She was paying a huge physical, emotional, and motivational price for the benefits of "being right" and harboring revenge fantasies. Yet the rage did not much respond to the tools we gave Sara and it started to become a huge roadblock to her healing.

Before so much misfortune had befallen her, Sara had had a daily meditation practice. She spoke of wanting to return to it and we encouraged her do so. She began sitting quietly in the mornings, following her breathing and simply "being with" whatever thoughts and feelings emerged. Rage was chief among these. She would sit for thirty minutes each morning seething with anger, bitterness, and hostility. "Not," she noted wryly, "what the Buddha probably did."

We suggested a change of venue. It was midsummer and we suggested Sara do her morning meditation on a bench at a local park. On the first morning she sat down, closed her eyes, and felt the old rage and aggression bubbling to the surface. Then she heard a songbird in the tree above her. Children's laughter drifted over from the playground. Sarah felt the warmth of the sun on her skin. A gentle breeze blew through her hair. She decided to continue following her breath and, for the first time in two years, began to feel stirrings of contentment. "Not happiness, exactly," she told us, "but just being okay with things. I realized my memories, thoughts, and feelings—like the sounds I was hearing, the sun, the breezes—arose and went away. I noticed for the first time there was a thinking part of me that had lots of opinions about life and a simpler, *present* part, there before any thinking at all. Staying with my simpler self I felt more and more peaceful, content—even grateful for the big picture of life."

After many months of intense suffering Sara's awareness began, flowerlike, to reopen as she sat in the morning sunlight. The fact pattern of her life remained exactly the same. But she found herself taking new positions in these facts. As we worked with her afterward Sara realized that rage was her way of refusing to accept her "new normal." Rage kept her vicariously living her old life, holding on to what she once had, refusing entirely to let it go. Now sitting in her simpler self she realized whether she held on or not, *all things* continually come and go. Sara decided to embrace this fundamental aspect of reality and with it a new experience of her past, present, and future. She began returning phone calls from photography clients. She made an appointment to be fitted with a prosthetic limb. She began working with a financial advisor to negotiate a payoff of her medical debt and reestablish herself on sound economic footing.

EXPERIMENT XXI

ᘜ Opening the Flower of Awareness

Step One: Take out your lab book and date this entry. Write down and rate the intensity of any symptom, including numbness, you'd like to reset.

Step Two: Find a quiet place indoors or out where you will not be disturbed by others. Set a timer for fifteen minutes and sit comfortably upright. Lower or close your eyes and focus on the diaphragmatic breathing you learned in Experiment II.

Step Three: Notice what thoughts and emotions come up, hang around, and move on. Notice as well what you are hearing, physically experiencing, smelling, and so on.

Step Four: When the timer goes off, re-rate the intensity of the original symptom and write down and rate any other positive or negative emotions that came up for you during this time.

Step Five: If this experiment seems to help you may want to repeat it daily for a week or two and measure the effects of dosing yourself with these several hours of awareness.

6

Belief

The Heart of the Matter

In chapter 1 of this book we looked at how belief sets the foundation for our lives. We believe the sun will rise tomorrow morning—and everything follows from that. Should that belief change you can imagine how our thoughts, feelings, and behaviors would experience a hard reset! Chapter 1 looked, too, at how most of our beliefs—our belief in gravity for instance—help us live happy, productive lives. Our belief in such things as the value of clean air and water produces thoughts and feelings that motivate us personally and collectively to act in ways that protect us and add value to our lives.

Unhelpful beliefs do just the opposite. They endanger our wellness and subtract value from our lives because, when they are triggered, they produce the negative thoughts, feelings, and self-sabotaging behaviors typical of conditions such as PTSD. Let's review how this occurs:

1. A traumatic event produces changes in the body, brain, and belief system.
2. When triggered by outside events a new unhelpful belief produces distorted, negative thoughts.
3. Distorted thinking produces unhealthy negative emotion and may activate the sympathetic nervous system.

4. Unhealthy negative emotion drives self-sabotaging behavior.
5. Self-sabotaging behavior confirms the new unhelpful belief.

You may remember Mary, the wilderness guide who was assaulted by a client during a trek in the backcountry. After the assault her belief about men changed. For her entire life until that point Mary had believed that men, like women, were mostly kind, generous people she could rely on in times of need. Even complete strangers had impressed her with their gallantry. After being attacked Mary began believing that many, perhaps most, men might be like her attacker—dangerous predators best avoided and kept at bay. This new belief was triggered when Mary was around men. Thinking she was in grave danger Mary would panic and flee for home and safety. Her brain began connecting the dots between avoidance and safety, and Mary's belief that fleeing from men was keeping her safe was thus "proven" to her time and again.

Belief, then, is the ground of thinking. Thoughts do not randomly appear out of the ether but arise predictably from underlying beliefs. Believing the sun will rise, we think in certain directions. Believing most men are dangerous predators, Mary had certain thoughts and not others. And while negative thoughts come and go depending on circumstances—*He's going to attack me! I have to get out of here!*—beliefs travel with us twenty-four/seven, usually beneath our conscious radar. Can you identify an unhelpful belief that would produce the two thoughts mentioned above? They might both spring from the belief *Most men are dangerous predators.* Without this underlying belief these thoughts would seldom arise. If they did arise it would be in response to a real threat. They would not, in other words, be negative thoughts but helpful, protective ones.

Albert Ellis noticed this connection between unhelpful beliefs and distorted thinking. He frequently created lists of irrational, or what he described as "nutty," beliefs that produced the negative thoughts that made his patients feel worthless, anxious, hopeless, and angry. Here are some beliefs from one such list:[1]

The past is all-important and because something once strongly affected one's life, it should indefinitely have the same effect.

If something is, or may be, dangerous or fearsome, one should be terribly concerned about it.

Human unhappiness is externally caused and people have little or no ability to control their sorrows and disturbances.

It is easier to avoid than to face certain life difficulties and self-responsibilities.

One should be dependent on others and need someone stronger than oneself on whom to rely.

One should become quite upset over other people's problems and disturbances.

Human happiness can be achieved by inertia and inaction.

Are any of these—or some version of them—beliefs you currently hold? In our work with trauma patients around the world, such beliefs keep surfacing. They seem less cultural artifacts than expressions of the human genome. Something about our hardwiring produces such beliefs after bad things happen to us. Perhaps it's not so different from the fact that when we're cut we bleed. Certain vulnerabilities just seem to come with the human condition.

FINGER POINTING

One way to identify our own unhelpful beliefs is to work backward from the negative thoughts that arise from them. Our thoughts are like fingers pointing back to their origins in our belief system. Finger pointing works like this: Begin with a negative thought such as *He is going to attack me.* Now ask yourself, *How do I know this is true?* We'll then find one or more unhelpful beliefs like *Most men are dangerous predators* or *Because that's what always happens to me.* These might represent our personal versions of Ellis's irrational belief that *The past is all-important and because something once strongly affected one's life, it should indefinitely have the same effect.*

Notice that unhelpful beliefs are oftentimes distorted in the same way negative thoughts arising from them are distorted. *Because that's what always happens to me* contains a number of distortions we've looked at together. Can you identify some of them? (Refer to the list on page 55.)

Perhaps you recognized clairvoyance, truthiness, and telescopy in the belief that *This always happens to me.* Just as these distortions are chinks in the armor of our negative thoughts, they are leverage points we can use to transform unhelpful beliefs into helpful, life-giving beliefs. Life-giving beliefs, when triggered, produce clear thinking and positive emotion that in turn drives productive, creative, self-rewarding behavior.

EXPERIMENT XXII

℞ Finger Pointing

Step One: Write down a distorted thought that the Drill Down exercise has identified as the source of an unhealthy negative emotion.

Step Two: Ask yourself, *How do I know this is so?*

Step Three: Write down the unhelpful belief or beliefs that come to mind.

Step Four: Write down the distortions you see in this unhelpful belief.

BELIEVE WHAT YOU WANT

Toward the end of his life the twentieth-century Austrian philosopher Ludwig Wittgenstein wrote a little book titled *On Certainty*. In it he looked at the process by which we come to "know" things. The process, in other words, by which we construct beliefs about ourselves, others, and the world. "But doesn't it come out here," Wittgenstein wrote, "that such knowledge is related to a *decision*?"[2]

Wittgenstein sees something important here. Again and again in our work with traumatized patients we've seen their brains make a *deci-*

sion to believe something. *Men are dangerous predators. There's no hope for me. I'm a worthless human being and everyone knows it.* Belief is not imposed on us by outside events nor is it entirely inculcated into us by teachers, parents, or society. There is always an important element of choice present. No one, not even ourselves, can force us to believe something we don't agree to believe.

This is extraordinarily good news! If we hold unhelpful beliefs—and indeed we all do—we can choose to transform them into helpful, life-giving beliefs. We can *decide* to believe whatever we want. Belief is as pliable as our vision of the future; we can choose to see any future whatsoever. Once we decommission an unhelpful belief it will no longer produce the thought patterns that drive the kind of unhealthy negative feelings and self-sabotaging behaviors that used to "prove" the validity of the unhelpful belief.

Perhaps you can see how working at the level of belief gives the greatest "bang for our CBT buck." If we're only working on distorted thoughts, without addressing the ground of those thoughts, we can end up playing a game of "whack-a-mole" with such thinking for a long time—as we defeat one thought, another pops up to take its place. But when we reset an unhelpful belief the distorted thoughts it produces will generally take care of themselves. Like weeds deprived of soil they will wither and die on their own.

BELIEVING WHAT SHE WANTS: A CASE STUDY

Remember Saleena, the schoolgirl shamed on her first day of school? On that terrible morning Saleena's brain adopted a new belief: *I must always please others before I have any thought of myself.* After courageously starting exposure work in the direction of turning toward not away from conflict, Saleena identified this belief and decided she wanted to reset it. Let's look together at how she did this, using the tools you now have learned.

Step One: Hidden Wisdom

Saleena wrote the unhelpful belief *I must always please others before I have any thought of myself* atop a page in her lab book. Next she wrote the distortions she found in it, the benefits of holding this belief, and the nice things these benefits said about her as a human being. Figure 6.1 shows what Saleena's Hidden Wisdom sheet looked like.

BELIEF: *I must always please others*

Distortions: 1. *Truthiness*

2. *Secret Judge*

3. *Mirroring*

4. *Perfectionism*

Benefits of holding this belief:

1. *It keeps me focused on others*

2. *It helps me avoid conflict*

3. *People like me more*

Good things being focused on others says about me:

1. *I am generous*

2. *I am curious about others*

Good things avoiding conflict says about me:

1. *I want to get along with others*

2. *I care about others' feelings*

Good things wanting to be liked says about me:

1. *I am friendly*

2. *I value warm human connections*

Figure 6.1. Saleena's Hidden Wisdom

Step Two: Price It

Next Saleena did the Price It exercise as shown in figure 6.2.

Considering her numbers, Saleena saw this belief represented an overpayment with suffering for the benefits her belief conferred. She decided she was ready for a new, life-giving belief.

<table>
<tr><td colspan="2">BELIEF: I must always please others</td></tr>
</table>

Benefits of the Belief	Price I Pay
1. Keeps me focused on others	1. Anxiety
2. Helps me avoid conflict	2. Depression
3. People like me more	3. Resentment
	4. Loneliness
	5. Not getting what I want
	6. Having others ignore me
25	*89*

Figure 6.2. Saleena's Price It

Step Three: New Deal

In a column on the left side of a lab book page Saleena wrote the benefits of believing *I must always please others before I have a thought about myself.* She then wrote down her backtalk to each of these benefits. Figure 6.3 (page 108) shows a section of her work.

Step Four: Cognitive Tools

Saleena was now ready to work on a cognitive reset of her belief. First she used the Kernel of Truth tool to capture what she might want to keep about the old, unhelpful belief. She decided that while it was indeed pleasurable to please others, this by itself was a poor basis for real intimacy. She next reached out to a friend whose ease with others Saleena admired. Together they played doubles. She and her friend co-constructed a new belief that Saleena liked the sound of: *I can choose to be my real self in relationship. This will produce the most real pleasure for all concerned.*

BELIEF: I must always please others	
Benefits of the Belief	**Backtalk**
1. Keeps me focused on others	1. Actually I am very focused on myself, trying extremely hard not to say or do anything that might upset others.
2. Helps me avoid conflict	2. Disagreement is probably an important part of healthy relationships. Maybe I can learn to disagree with others in a way that works for me and for them.
3. People like me more	3. I don't think people ever get to know the real me. They're just getting a people-pleasing machine and they probably pick that up.

Figure 6.3. Saleena's New Deal

Step Five: Behavioral Tools

Saleena was now ready behaviorally to install her new belief. We invited her to begin with some in vitro work. We asked her to act as if she believed she could be real with *us*. She took a deep breath, teared up a bit, then bravely agreed. Saleena then told us that while our work together was lifesaving, she sometimes felt rubbed the wrong way by things we did or said. We asked for particular examples, and they came pouring out! One of our yoga sets aggravated her asthma. She resented things another treatment group member had said recently. Certain of our CBT tools seemed like a complete waste of time. She paused here and again took a deep breath, looking at us with wide eyes.

We were *so proud* of Saleena that day and immediately told her so.

She had just become real to us in a whole new way and we *really liked* the real Saleena! We said it made complete sense that some of what we or other group members said would turn her off or seem irrelevant. We're not clones of each other and no thing or person is everyone's cup of tea. Saleena began weeping and told us this was the first time since age five she'd risked presenting her real self to anyone. A part of her couldn't believe she was "getting away" with doing this—that we didn't reject or punish her for telling us who she really was.

Saleena found this session life changing. The next step was to go in vivo with her work. Her real-life bravery produced much the same results. Saleena's brain kept careful track of all this data. Two weeks later we asked Saleena how much she believed *I can choose to be my real self in relationship: this will produce the greatest real pleasure for all concerned.* "One thousand percent," she promptly replied. We then asked how much she now believed *I must always please others before I have a thought about myself.* Saleena did a double take, then burst out laughing. We couldn't have hoped for a better answer.

EXPERIMENT XXIII

🐚 Believe What You Want

Following the outline presented above, select an unhelpful belief you'd like to transform into a helpful one. Saleena selected tools that seemed most relevant to her and you can do the same. The Hidden Wisdom, Price It, and New Deal tools will be important starting points. If you talk back resoundingly to the unhelpful belief's benefits, you too will be a candidate to move on to the cognitive then behavioral resets needed to identify the new belief and start acting as if it were so. If your backtalk is less than convincing it might be better to keep that belief for now and look for some other belief you might want to reset.

7

Yoga

Embodied Wellness

In chapter 2 we presented the way the body and brain are affected by trauma and ways in which CBT, yoga, and meditation improve trauma symptoms. We will now present the yogic teachings and techniques that have helped so many patients in our Integrative Trauma Recovery Program. First, here is a little background.

A BRIEF HISTORY OF YOGA

Archeological evidence links the origins of yoga to 1500 BCE and the Indus Valley civilization, which is present-day India and Pakistan. The Sanskrit word *yoga* comes from the root *yug* (as in "yoke"), meaning "to join together" or "union." One interpretation of the word is the spiritual union whereby an individual's consciousness becomes united with the Infinite Consciousness, the Divine Consciousness, or the Reality underlying the universe.[1] This union is also called the state of "enlightenment."

While yoga is a spiritual practice for millions of people it may also be practiced therapeutically. If we are seeking a sense of inner peace, balance, and wholeness, these results can be obtained regardless of the intention of the practice. Patanjali, an ancient yogic philosopher, taught that every human being is by nature balanced and whole.[2] The practice of yoga is one way to align ourselves with this inner wholeness and to promote physical and emotional healing.

YOGA ANATOMY AND PHYSIOLOGY

We have discussed the ways in which yoga decreases PTSD symptoms from the Western scientific perspective. The yogic perspective is different from, though in many ways parallel to, the Western way of thinking about the structural and functional organization of the body. In Western anatomy and physiology we think of the body as being composed of various interconnected systems such as the immune system, the endocrine system, the circulatory system, the nervous system, the reproductive system, and the digestive system. Yogic anatomy also refers to interconnected systems such as *nadis* (channels) and *chakras* and is based on the concept of subtle energy. This subtle energy has been recognized for thousands of years through many cultures and been given many names. The yogic tradition calls it *prana*. It is known as *chi* in traditional Chinese medicine. It was *pneuma* in ancient Greece and *ankh* in ancient Egypt. Native American cultures have their own names for this primal energy. In Navajo it is known as *nilch'i,* in Inuit *sila,* and in Iroquois *orenda*. It is oftentimes also referred to as "life force" or "bioenergy."

Breath is a key component of many yoga practices and a main component of the yoga exercises and meditations presented in this book. Breath is important because it carries the life force or subtle energy— the prana. Prana moves through the nadis (channels), of which there are 72,000 described in yogic texts. The three main energy channels are the *ida,* the *pingala,* and the *sushumna*. The sushumna, the central channel, begins at the base of the spine and ends at the top of the head. The ida and pingala also begin at the base of the spine with the ida on the left and the pingala on the right. The most common description of these channels, based on the interpretation of the yogic texts, is that the ida and pingala wind around the sushumna like a helix with the ida ending at the left nostril and the pingala ending at the right nostril.

The ida and the pingala have unique and opposite qualities. The ida has cooling and receptive characteristics and is associated with calmness, sensitivity, and empathy. The pingala has warming and projective characteristics and is associated with vigor, alertness, willpower, concentration, and readiness for action. These subtle-energy structures have not yet been identified by current imaging technologies. However they resemble the sympathetic and parasympathetic nervous systems in Western anatomy and the *yin* and *yang* in traditional Chinese medicine. The ida and pingala—like the sympathetic and parasympathetic nervous systems or Chinese yin and yang—have opposite qualities yet are interdependent.

Chakras (wheels) are another component of yogic anatomy and there are seven different chakras located along the spine. In the West chakras are linked to specific nerve plexuses or endocrine glands such as the adrenals, thyroid, and pituitary. However, yogic texts locate the chakras in the energetic rather than the physical body.

YOGIC BREATHING

The flow of prana, carried by the breath, maintains balance in the body and is a key to good health. The flow of prana is disrupted when the nadis that carry this energy are blocked or when the breath itself is disrupted due to dysregulation effects of trauma. Yogic breathing practices can keep prana flowing through the nadis and help restore health and balance to the whole body. We will now consider a number of breath patterns—and their functions—that you will utilize while doing the yoga presented in this and other chapters.

Long, Deep Breathing

Long, deep breathing is a relaxing breath used throughout yogic practice to activate the parasympathetic nervous system. Just changing our breath from shallow and fast to long and deep generally results in feelings of relaxation. This breath pattern utilizes the full capacity of the lungs. It aids in emotional and physical healing and helps break thought patterns that drive insecurity and fear. It also builds capacity to manage difficult emotion and supports clarity and patience.[3] A recent study found that the benefits of long, deep breathing continued after the exercise itself had ended and normal breathing had resumed.[4]

Cannon Breath

This breath is used in the Elementary Adjustment of the Brain meditation presented later in this chapter. Here the lips form a tight circle and air is inhaled and exhaled rapidly through the mouth. The inhalation and exhalation are equal in depth and intensity. This breath is said to aid digestion, increase inner energy, boost the immune system, and cleanse the body.[5] Breathing through the rounded mouth is also believed to help release shame, guilt, and fear.[6]

Left Nostril Breathing

This breath is used in one of the exercises in the yoga set Kriya to Still Nerves, Shakes, Anxiety, and Tension presented below. It, too, is a traditional breath pattern used in many yoga practices. Because the ida energy channel ends at the left nostril, breathing through the left nostril supports experiences of calmness, sensitivity, and empathy associated with that channel.

Segmented Breathing

Segmented breathing is another classic pattern. Different segmented breaths have different effects and all help bring the nervous system back into balance. An eight-part inhalation paired with an eight-part exhalation is a calming and centering breath pattern. It is taught in Pauri Kriya in chapter 9 and in exercise 1 of the Kriya to Still Nerves, Shakes, Anxiety, and Tension. The breath pattern taught in Shabad Kriya in chapter 8 has a twenty-two-beat pattern with a segmented inhale and exhale. Research has shown this breath pattern to contribute to healthy sleep.[7]

THE QUALITIES OF VARIOUS
YOGA MUDRAS (HAND POSITIONS)

Mudras, or seals, are hand positions that seal and direct energy flow and cultivate a particular state of mind. Each area of the hand corresponds to a certain part of the body or brain related to different emotions and behaviors.[8] A simple demonstration of the effect of a mudra is to bring your palms together in "prayer pose," palms pressed together with the thumbs at the sternum. This makes most of us feel more mentally collected. Alternatively, clenching the hand into a fist (not a yogic mudra!) brings us to a less calm state of mind.

The mudra that is commonly used during meditation and while relaxing between yoga exercises is *gyan* mudra. This mudra and other mudras that will be used in Pauri Kriya are described in table 7.1.[9]

Table 7.1. Mudras Used in Pauri Kriya

Name of Mudra	Illustration	Description	Qualities
Gyan Mudra (Seal of Knowledge)		The tip of the thumb touches the tip of the index finger	Knowledge, wisdom, receptivity, and calmness
Shuni Mudra (Seal of Patience)		The tip of the thumb touches the tip of the middle finger	Patience, discernment, and commitment
Surya Mudra (Seal of Life)		The tip of the thumb touches the tip of the ring finger	Vitality and energy of life
Buddhi Mudra (Seal of Mental Clarity)		The tip of the thumb touches the tip of the little finger	Ability to communicate

KUNDALINI YOGA

The yoga exercises and meditations in this book are from a particular style of yoga called Kundalini Yoga as taught by Yogi Bhajan®, which incorporates body postures, breath, mantra (chant), and meditation. The exercises and meditations were taught by Yogi Bhajan, who founded the 3HO Foundation (Healthy, Happy, Holy Organization) in 1969 to bring Kundalini Yoga to a broader population. Kundalini Yoga as taught by Yogi Bhajan is a comprehensive style of yoga with an emphasis on psychological and spiritual growth as well as physical health (referred to throughout this book as Kundalini Yoga).[10]

Kundalini Yoga is so called because it is based on the flow of kundalini energy. Kundalini energy is considered the energy of consciousness. It is the creative potential of the human being. This energy is said to sit dormant at the sushumna at the base of the spine. The practice of Kundalini Yoga allows this energy to flow by removing energy blockages in the nadis and opening the chakras. Kundalini energy also activates the pineal gland in the brain. According to Yogi Bhajan, when the kundalini energy begins to flow, "A new clarity accompanies your perception, thought, and intuition . . . a person becomes totally and wholly aware. That is why it is called 'the yoga of awareness.'"[11]

We teach this style of yoga as it was taught by Yogi Bhajan so that patients receive the full intended effect and benefit of the yogic technology. As you saw in the descriptions of the breathing exercises above, different breaths have different effects. The same holds true for the physical exercises and mantras (words that are chanted) that are used. Our research and that of others has found that the yoga exercises and meditations presented below help reduce trauma symptoms and promote an experience of physical and emotional wellness.[12]

THE IMPORTANCE OF MANTRA IN KUNDALINI YOGA

Mantra, or chanting, has been practiced through time in virtually every spiritual and religious tradition. The word "mantra" comes from the Sanskrit *man* (meaning mind) and *trang* (wave or projection). Mantra is the creative projection of the mind through sound.[13] Mantras are formulas that alter the patterns of the mind (including thoughts) and the chemistry of the brain. Perhaps this is why mantras have been so widely used across cultures. Chanting mantras has physiological effects, in part by stimulating meridian points on the roof of the mouth. You may be familiar with meridian points stimulated by needles during acupuncture. The meridian points on the roof of the mouth are stimulated with the tongue during chanting. There are eighty-four such points located in the mouth. Thirty-two pairs (sixty-four points) are along the inside of the teeth. The other twenty points are in a "U" shape on the central part of the hard palate. According to yogic teachings, when the tongue touches these points during chanting it stimulates the hypothalamus and the pituitary glands to balance the endocrine (hormone) system.

KRIYAS IN KUNDALINI YOGA

Kundalini Yoga is composed of *kriyas*. Kriya translates from Sanskrit as "completed action." A kriya is a sequence of postures, breath, and mantra integrated to allow the manifestation of a particular effect.[14] Kriyas are often called "yoga sets," six to ten exercises practiced for several minutes each, with a few minutes of relaxation in between each one. A kriya may also be an individual exercise/meditation using a particular mudra and involving a focus on the breath or mantra. Meditations are usually done following the deep relaxation after a yoga set, though they may be done by themselves. Finally, some meditations, such as Elementary Adjustment of the Brain, consist of a few exercises with movement.

Yogi Bhajan stressed the importance of doing all of the parts of a kriya together in the same order as he originally taught in order to have the intended effect (thus we do not pick and choose exercises from a kriya to do individually). An analogy would be getting a prescription for medication from a doctor that comes with specific instructions. If we don't follow these instructions we might not receive the drug's full intended benefit.

LENGTH OF MEDITATIONS IN KUNDALINI YOGA

Yogi Bhajan describes specific lengths of meditation (and exercises in a kriya) needed to obtain certain effects.[15] These times are as follows:

Three minutes affects circulation (blood) and the electromagnetic field

Eleven minutes changes the glandular system and the nerves

Twenty-two minutes balances and coordinates the three minds (positive, negative, and neutral mind)

Thirty-one minutes affects all of the cells and rhythms of the body and all the layers of the mind's projection

Sixty-two minutes changes the grey matter of the brain and integrates the subconscious "shadow mind" and the outer projection

You will see some of these times in the kriyas and meditations presented in this and the following chapters.

Now that you have an understanding of the fundamentals of Kundalini Yoga we'll look together at the kriyas. Here are some tips on maximizing your benefit from these ancient practices.

Guidelines for Practicing Kundalini Yoga

1. Wear comfortable clothes and choose a time and place where you won't be disturbed. Ideally yoga is done barefoot. This also facilitates the flow of energy.

2. Unless otherwise specified, all exercises are done with the eyes closed. This helps provide greater focused attention on the exercise and the breath. If you prefer to keep your eyes open, you can focus on a point in front of you or on the floor.

3. If sitting cross-legged on the floor is uncomfortable you may do all of the yoga seated in a chair. Sitting on a cushion on the floor is also fine. If seated in a chair maintain a straight spine and keep both feet on the floor. Keeping the spine straight is important and will allow the proper breathing. For this reason, practicing on a couch or reclining chair is not recommended.

4. Relaxation is an important part of a Kundalini Yoga practice. In the Kriya to Still Nerves, Shakes, Anxiety, and Tension and in the Elementary Adjustment of the Brain you will be relaxing between the exercises. Unless otherwise specified, relax from one to three minutes between each exercise. If the exercise is short (three minutes) as in the Elementary Adjustment of the Brain, then the relaxation will also be short (one minute). If the exercise is longer, such as eleven minutes in the first exercise of the Kriya to Still Nerves, Shakes, Anxiety, and Tension, then the relaxation may be three minutes. When the entire yoga set is finished you'll take a longer period of relaxation, which may be ten to fifteen minutes. You may need to build up to this length of relaxation and that is fine. Deep relaxation creates and maintains balance in the body and is important for healing the nervous and glandular systems.[16]

You may relax in any position you find comfortable. In the shorter periods of relaxation between exercises in a yoga set you may sit in a cross-legged position. For the longer periods at the end of a yoga set you'll relax in *shavaasana* (corpse pose), which is done lying on your back with the arms to the sides, palms facing up, and ankles uncrossed. If you wish, you may also lie down between exercises in a set to relax. This might be helpful as all of the exercises presented below are done in a cross-legged position; lying down to relax between them allows you to stretch your legs.

5. While practicing yoga, Kundalini practitioners cover their heads with a natural fiber cloth such as cotton. Covering the head provides a sense of containment and focus.[17] If your hair is long enough to be pulled up, it can be gathered and coiled at the top of the head. Yogi Bhajan taught that coiling the hair in this way aids in raising the kundalini energy.[18]

   Covering your head is optional. We invite you to add this to the series of experiments you have done throughout this book. You can try practicing Kundalini Yoga and meditations with and without a head covering (such as a handkerchief) to see if you notice a difference. Sometimes students who are particularly sensitive to the flow of energy may develop a headache when doing certain meditations. In all our years of teaching Kundalini Yoga we have only seen this happen with one student during her home practice. Wearing a head covering while doing yoga eliminated her headaches.

6. When practicing yoga or meditations you may feel negative emotions. This is normal. Yoga works on areas of the brain that regulate emotions. If this happens just allow these emotions to come up and continue to focus on the breath as they move through your system. Pausing an exercise may also help as you bring yourself back to awareness of the breath and into the present moment.

TO START A KUNDALINI YOGA SET OR MEDITATION

Before doing any Kundalini Yoga set or meditation, we begin by chanting a specific mantra. We call this process Tuning In.

The words to the mantra are *Ong namo guru dev namo*. This means "I bow to the creative wisdom. I bow to the divine teacher within."

An easy way to learn this mantra is to watch a video demonstration at www.integrative-trauma-recovery.com.

Here is a written description of the pronunciation:

Ong: This syllable sounds like "song" without the "s" and with an emphasis on the "ng," which produces a vibration on the roof of the mouth.

Namo: The first part of *namo* is short and rhymes with "hum." The long "o," as in "go," is held longer.

Guru: "Gu" sounds like "good" without the "d" and "ru" rhymes with "true." The *r* is rolled slightly.

Dev: *Dev* rhymes with "gave."

~ Chanting the Mantra to Tune In

To chant this mantra, sit with the spine straight. You may sit in a chair with your feet on the floor or sit cross-legged on the floor. Bring your hands together at the center of the chest as pictured. Your palms are together with a few pounds of pressure. Your

Posture for Tuning In

thumbs are against the sternum and your fingers point upward. Close your eyes and focus them at the brow point (the point above your nose and between your eyebrows). This posture has a calming neutralizing effect on the body and helps to focus the mind.

Inhale deeply and chant "Ong namo guru dev namo." You will chant this mantra three times, taking a deep breath between each repetition. Then inhale deeply. Continue to focus your eyes at the brow point as you hold the breath for a few moments. Then exhale and relax.

Continue with a Few Minutes of Long, Deep Breathing

Long, deep breathing is an important part of any yoga practice. It can be done between the exercises of a yoga set and is an opportunity to focus on the breath and be aware of the effect of the exercises. We tend to breathe shallowly and from the upper part of the chest when we are anxious or nervous. Long, deep breathing is a much more complete breath and results in a calm and relaxed state.

It is helpful to have a visual image of the parts of body involved in breathing. The upper section of the torso is the thoracic cavity. It is surrounded by the ribcage and contains the heart and the lungs. The lower section is the abdominal cavity. It contains several organs including the stomach, liver, and small intestines. The diaphragm is the domed-shape muscle dividing these two cavities. When you inhale the diaphragm dome flattens and extra space is created to expand the lungs above it. When you exhale the diaphragm moves back up into the dome shape and pushes out the air from the lower lungs. Long, deep breathing utilizes three parts of the lungs: lower, middle, and upper.

ॐ Long, Deep Breathing

Begin by sitting with your spine straight. You may either sit cross-legged on the floor or in a chair with your feet flat on the floor. As you inhale let the belly relax so that the abdomen expands, then feel the ribs expand outward, and finally feel the collarbone lift slightly. As you exhale feel the collarbone come back down, the ribs move back in, and the navel point move back toward the spine.

Any time you do long, deep breathing, you may add the silent mantra *Sat nam* (rhymes with "but Mom"). *Sat nam* means "Truth is my identity." Mentally repeat "sat" as you inhale and "nam" as you exhale. This mantra has the ability to break or interrupt thought patterns and clear the subconscious mind.[19]

YOGA SET AND MEDITATION FOR TRAUMA SYMPTOMS

Below are directions for doing the yoga set Kriya to Still Nerves, Shakes, Anxiety, and Tension and the meditation Elementary Adjustment of the Brain. You can also see these exercises described and demonstrated on videos at www.integrative-trauma-recovery.com.

These are two fundamental yoga components of the Integrative Trauma Recovery Program that significantly reduced PTSD symptoms and improved sleep in our research study.[20] The Elementary Adjustment of the Brain was the program's home-meditation practice.

This yoga set and meditation may be practiced individually or in combination. If they are done together either may be done first with a relaxation between the two. The relaxation is described above in the Guidelines section (see pages 117–19). Note that there are also brief relaxations (one to three minutes) between the exercises, as described previously.

The exercises in the Kriya to Still Nerves, Shakes, Anxiety, and Tension need to be done together in order as written so that the maximum effect is achieved. Similarly the three exercises in the Elementary Adjustment of the Brain must also be done together and in order. However, the times of each exercise may be shortened. When they are shortened, they are reduced proportionally. For example, in the

Elementary Adjustment of the Brain meditation, you may start by doing each of the three exercises for one minute each and over several days of practice build up to three minutes each. If you reduced the times in half for the Kriya to Still Nerves, Shakes, Anxiety, and Tension, you would do the first exercise for five and a half minutes and the other exercise for two and a half minutes. Or you may want to start with three and a half minutes for the first exercise and about one and a half minutes for the rest.

Kriya to Still Nerves, Shakes, Anxiety, and Tension*

Hand Position for Exercise 1[†]

Exercise 1

Sit in cross-legged position. Place the thumb and index finger together with the tips touching (gyan mudra). Place the wrists just under the ear lobes with a slight pressure against the neck. Inhale in eight equal, separate parts and exhale in eight equal, separate parts. This will be like inhaling in eight sniffs in and exhaling in eight sniffs. Continue for eleven minutes.

---

*Kundalini Yoga as taught by Yogi Bhajan®
[†]Note that all hand-position images are as if you are looking at another person (not looking down at your own hands), as with all other exercise images.

ༀ Exercise 2

Sit in cross-legged position. Place the left palm facing out from
the chest. Place the right hand facing the chest. Bring the fingers
together. Curl the fingers of both hands so the hands form a
fist. Your forearms are parallel to the floor. With the right thumb
extended, close off the right nostril. Breathe long and deep through
the left nostril for five minutes as you pull your hands apart with a
slight pressure.

↬ Exercise 3

Part 1

Sit in cross-legged position. The hands are in fists with the palms down. Place the left hand on the floor in front of the body; the right hand is behind you.

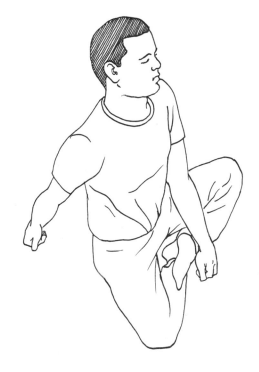

Part 2

Inhale and raise the arms parallel to the ground, hands still in fists with the palms facing down. Exhale and lower the arms to the starting position. Continue this motion for five minutes.

ᘓ Exercise 4

Part 1

Arms are to the sides with the elbows bent. Tilt the hands back so the palms face upward. The fingers are separated equally and slightly curved as if each hand is holding a ball. Breathe long and deep.

Part 2

On the inhale, close the fists, and clench and push out the chest, then exhale and open the fists to the starting position; relax the chest. Continue this motion slowly and powerfully for five minutes.

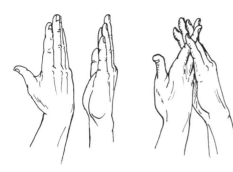

Hand Position Step 1   Hand Position Step 2

Hand Position Step 3

Hand Position Step 4

ॐ Exercise 5

Hand position step 1: Place both hands in front of the chest with palms facing each other. Then twist the right hand counterclockwise so both palms face to the right.

Hand position step 2: Interlace the fingers of each hand with the left little finger outside of the right index finger, and the right little finger outside of the left index finger.

Hand position step 3: Bring the elbows up so the fingers remain interlaced with the left palm facing out and the right palm facing toward you.

Hand position step 4: Place the right thumb on top of the left little finger and the left thumb under the right little finger.

Final position: Bring the level of the hands to the throat. Pull slightly on the hands holding a gentle tension. Chant "Sat nam" in this position for five minutes. For this mantra the "sat" is drawn out for a longer time and the "nam" is short: "Saaaaaaaaaaaaaaaaaaaaaaat naam."

At the end of this series of exercises, relax completely.

ᏗᏬ Elementary Adjustment of the Brain*

The following elementary adjustment "will change the third layer of the neurons in a single rhythm and will regulate the first ring under the stem of the brain."[21]

Hand Position for Exercise 1

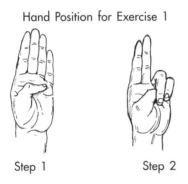

Step 1   Step 2

Part A

ᏗᏬ Exercise 1

Part A

Sit in cross-legged position with the spine straight. The thumb touches the mound under the little finger. The ring and the little fingers bend over the thumb, holding it in place. The index and middle fingers are straight. Bend your elbows, keeping the forearms parallel to the ground. The hands are held at the level of the heart center with the palms downward and the index and middle fingers of each hand pointing at each other.

Make an "O" of your mouth, inhale through the rounded mouth, and exhale forcefully through the nose. The force of the exhale will cause your nose to wrinkle.

*Kundalini Yoga as taught by Yogi Bhajan® April 22, 1993

Part B

As you exhale through the nose, the hands and forearms move outward so that the index and middle fingers point straight out away from you. When you inhale through the mouth, return to the original position. Focus your eyes on the tip of your nose. Continue for three minutes.

To finish: Inhale deeply, hold your breath for ten seconds while you lock your back molars and tighten all your muscles. Exhale forcefully with a cannon breath through the O-shaped mouth. Repeat this inhale/hold; tighten/exhale sequence two more times and relax.

This exercise will cause the entire back area of the head to vibrate. It will give oxygen directly to your brain, stimulate your pituitary, and totally fix the vibrator, which is the pineal gland. It is effective for relieving loss of memory, loss of feelings, and nightmares.

Part B

Hand Position for
Exercises 2 and 3

⁊꙰ Exercise 2

Sit in cross-legged position with a straight spine. Keep the index and middle fingers straight while you bend the little and ring fingers and lock them down with your thumb. Bend the elbows so that your forearms are pointing upward and the hands are near shoulder level with the index and middle fingers pointing straight up.

The breath is a rapid diaphragm breath through the rounded mouth. There will be a "hoo, hoo, hoo" sound similar to the sound baboons make. The diaphragm will move as fast as a hummingbird's wings. Rotate your hands in small outward circles as fast as you can, while you breathe rapidly through your rounded mouth. Continue for three minutes.

To finish: Inhale deeply, hold your breath for ten seconds while you tighten all your muscles and tightly press your lips together. Exhale forcefully with a cannon breath through the O-shaped mouth. Repeat this inhale/hold; tighten/exhale sequence two more times and then relax.

ᨓ Exercise 3

Keep your hands in the same position as in exercise 2. Stay in cross-legged position and hold your arms straight out to the sides, with the palms of the hands facing upward and the index and middle fingers pointing straight out. Twist your hands backward as far as you can. The inner elbow will face upward and be stretched toward the back as your hands twist. There will be a healing pain in the elbows. If the elbows are twisted properly, the chest will automatically press forward and the rib cage will lift. Hold this position breathing naturally. Continue for three minutes.

To finish: Inhale deeply, hold your breath for ten seconds while you lock your back molars, tighten all the muscles, and twist the elbows with maximum effort. Exhale forcefully with a cannon breath through the O-shaped mouth. Repeat this inhale/hold; tighten/exhale sequence two more times and relax.

Correctly done, this posture will cause the serum in the spine to change, bringing a renewed youthfulness and balance to the body.

Additional note about locking the back molars: Clenching the molars at the end of exercises 1 and 3 creates the ability to sustain new behaviors. It works on the temporal lobe to create stability and strength.[22] However, if you have any structural, jaw, or dental issues where clenching the molars would be a problem, then you would not do this.

You may practice this yoga set and meditation as often as you wish. We measured improvement in all PTSD symptom groups in the research study on our Integrative Trauma Recovery Program and we saw a significant correlation in the amount of home practice of the Elementary Adjustment of the Brain meditation and improvement in sleep. Those who practiced more often slept better.

As in the CBT exercises we have been teaching, you may perform the same kind of experiment with these yoga sets. Do this practice and note any changes in how you feel. You may even want to rate any symptoms on a scale of 1 to 100.

You have just learned two Kundalini Yoga kriyas for trauma symptoms. In the next chapter you will learn Shabad Kriya, which is an effective meditation for sleep.

8

Sleep Well

One of the more agonizing aspects of PTSD is the way it can disturb not only our waking hours but what should be our resting hours as well. The Centers for Disease Control and Prevention reports that up to one in three American adults has some level of sleep difficulty on any given night, but this number is markedly higher among those with PTSD: up to 90 percent of PTSD patients regularly have difficulty falling or staying asleep. Occasional sleepless nights happen to all of us. Chronic insomnia on the other hand is a medical condition that can stand alone but is often associated with other disorders, including anxiety, depression, and PTSD. We've already touched on nightmares and tools we can use to address them. In this chapter we'll present additional methods for addressing insomnia. Let's begin with an overview of our goal: healthy, restorative sleep.

NORMAL SLEEP STRUCTURE

Sleep proceeds through four consecutive stages, beginning with stage one or "light sleep," continuing through two "deep sleep" stages, and culminating in REM, the stage in which we dream. A complete journey through this cycle takes between one and two hours and is repeated a number of times through the night. The length of time we spend in each stage changes from cycle to cycle and also changes as we age. Infants spend half their sleep time in REM; adults spend about 20 percent of their time in REM and up to 50 percent in stage two.

While there is not yet an overarching theory of why we sleep there is an increasing body of data about sleep's benefits and the ways in which insufficient sleep hurts our bodies and minds. Insomnia impairs our memories, reduces attention span and problem-solving ability, and increases our risk of high blood pressure, weight gain, heart disease, depression, and anxiety. Research suggests better sleep correlates with better health at even the molecular level. As mentioned in chapter 2, telomeres are protective DNA sequences at the ends of our chromosomes. As we age telomeres shorten. Yet older adults who sleep well have telomere lengths comparable to middle-aged people.[1] Studies have shown sleep also clears the brain of the waste byproducts of cellular metabolism.[2] One such waste product, the protein beta-amyloid, is highly associated with Alzheimer's disease. We are increasingly appreciating the huge role sleep plays in human wellness and illness alike.

For good reason, then, the Geneva Convention—an international body of humanitarian rules relating to behavior during times of armed conflict—prohibits sleep deprivation as a prisoner interrogation technique: it truly is a form of torture. Taken to extremes it kills. The rare genetic disease fatal familial insomnia progresses from bouts of increasing sleeplessness to terminal wakefulness—a kind of waking coma state—that ends only with death. Happily most sleep problems are not of this order! When we are not consistently sleeping the eight hours or so we need to wake feeling rested, energized, and optimistic, we can remedy this state of affairs.

When they are not sleeping well many people try over-the-counter or prescription sleep aids. While these might help in the short term— after surgery, say, or while traveling through time zones—regular use of these medications creates new problems. One problem is tolerance; we'll typically stop responding to an initial dose and require more and more of the drug. Another problem is these substances don't create normal sleep. They tend to artificially produce one or two sleep stages but not a normal sleep cycle. As a result users often report feeling drugged, lethargic, or hung over the following morning and even throughout the entire next day.

Research studies have shown CBT, yoga, and meditation to be very effective in improving healthy sleep in people with insomnia. One study showed meditation to be as effective as sleep medication.[3] CBT has been found to be *more effective than sleep medication in the long term.*[4] Yoga and CBT help insomnia in the general population and have also been shown specifically to help PTSD-related insomnia.[5] Before looking at some of these natural, fast-acting, and medication-free approaches, let's turn our attention to another important aspect of healthy slumber—sleep hygiene.

SLEEP HYGIENE

Just as properly refrigerating perishable foods or washing our hands before eating promotes physical wellness, some simple bedtime habits greatly support sound sleep. Here are five basic guidelines:

1. Maintain a regular sleep/wake schedule. Vary no more than sixty minutes from your usual times on any given morning or night.
2. Avoid daytime naps. If you feel you must nap, do so for no more than forty minutes and no later than 4 p.m.
3. Moderate exercise before sunset and exposure to sunlight help your body's circadian rhythms synch with a normal sleep/wake cycle.
4. Create a sleep environment that is safe, quiet, dark, and physically comfortable. A supportive mattress and cool room temperature are both very important.
5. Avoid caffeine, alcohol, heavy meals, and electronic screens in the lead-up to bedtime. Quiet reading, a warm bath, or enjoyable conversation with loved ones make you an excellent candidate for stage one sleep.

Incorporating these guidelines will, more than anything else you can do, support consolidation of your sleep and promote sleep efficiency. Let's look more closely at these terms as they point to important aspects of normal sleep.

One way insomnia interrupts sleep is by fracturing it into abnormal segments throughout the night. It is normal to awaken briefly at the end of REM sleep. If we are waking at other times it is difficult to complete one normal sleep cycle and move on to the next. When we consolidate sleep we remove these abnormal awakenings and reset to healthy sleep architecture. Sleep efficiency is the ratio of time in bed to time asleep. None of us is 100 percent efficient when it comes to sleep. We all take some time to drift off, to get out of bed in the morning, and to be awake in the night after a cycle of REM sleep or to use the bathroom. Consider 90 percent efficiency a good goal. This would mean that for any ten hours in bed we'd be asleep nine of those hours.

Finding the Sandman

After going to bed we might find ourselves still awake at the end of what feels like a reasonable "nodding off" period. We might then start to fidget and fret, looking for our inner sandman and trying to "make" ourselves nod off to sleep. Some patients tell us they lie in bed for hours in this state, becoming increasingly "wired, tired—and awake." Yet trying to *make* ourselves sleep is like trying to *make* ourselves digest our food. Attempting consciously to force involuntary physiologic responses only interferes with their taking place.

Patients caught in this terrible cycle are unwittingly contributing to a common sleep problem we call "conditioned arousal." Remember reading in high school about the work of Russian physiologist Ivan Pavlov? Dr. Pavlov would ring a bell while feeding a dog and the animal would soon associate the sound of the bell with the presence of food. Once so "conditioned," the dog would begin to salivate upon hearing the bell, whether food was presented or not. The bell had now become an external cue for an involuntary physical response.

Exactly this pairing of stimulus and response happens throughout our lives. We walk into the kitchen at a certain time of day and smell a delicious meal cooking. As with Pavlov's dogs these stimuli (place, time, scent) cue an involuntary reaction. Or we walk into the bathroom simply to wash our hands and suddenly feel the urge to urinate. When we are sleeping normally this classical conditioning works in our favor. A particular time in the evening, room in our home, piece of furniture, and our position upon the piece of furniture cue stage-one sleep. We lie down, nature takes over, and we are well on our way to dreamland.

We now can see how lying awake in bed for extended times pairs the usual bedtime cues not with sleep but with wakefulness. We are classically conditioning ourselves to be insomniacs. Unfortunately here as elsewhere practice makes perfect! The more we train ourselves to be awake in bed, the better we get at it. We may then create the additional problem of developing fears and phobias around bedtime and the rest of our sleep lives. Insomniac patients sometimes tell us they start to get anxious in the late afternoon just anticipating their nightly ordeal with the missing sandman.

We can step out of this vicious conditioned arousal cycle in two ways presented below. Using either tool or both helps patients turn off nighttime wakefulness and, sometimes within only a few days, dramatically increase their sleep efficiency.

EXPERIMENT XXIV

☙ Finding the Sandman

Step One: If after going to bed (or after awakening in the night) you find yourself not returning to sleep, get out of bed. You may want to have by your bedside some warm, comfortable clothes and slippers.

Step Two: Leave the bedroom and engage in some quiet, relaxing activity. Make yourself a cup of herbal tea. Read a favorite book. Do some gentle stretching or one of the sleep-enhancing yoga exercises we'll describe below. Avoid electronic screens or other activities that will send a message to your brain that it's now time to be awake and at work.

Step Three: When you start yawning return to bed, focus on long, deep breathing, and enjoy the experience of drifting into stage-one sleep.

Restricting the Sandman

Another way to immediately increase sleep efficiency is to limit the sandman's range. With fewer places to hide we can more quickly find him. The experience of one of our patients demonstrates how this works.

As a young man Matt was injected at a hospital with a contaminated drug that nearly took his life. He eventually recovered but found himself with a number of neurologic problems and increasing difficulty sleeping. For two decades he struggled to regain a normal sleep life, trying sleeping pills, medical marijuana, and many other approaches. Some of these helped him for a while but all eventually lost their efficacy. When Matt came to us he had many unhelpful beliefs about himself and sleep and had conditioned himself to be awake about 60 percent of the time he was in bed. We first worked with Matt on his beliefs about sleep (we'll talk more about this below). We then explained the concept of conditioned arousal, which helped Matt see how for many years he had been contributing to his sleep problem. Matt agreed to begin restricting his sleep in the following way.

Matt had been going to bed about 10 p.m., lying awake for three hours, then sleeping on and off until finally getting out of bed, exhausted, at 10 a.m. the following morning. He calculated he was getting a total of five hours of sleep during this time. Matt's experiment began with setting 12:30 a.m. as his new bedtime. He figured that as he was never asleep before this time, he might as well stop conditioning himself to be awake. He also set his alarm for 8 a.m. and would leave his bed for the day at this time and go outside for a walk in the morning sun.

As you can imagine this new schedule represented a hard reset for Matt! Yet weary of many years of weariness, Matt stuck to the new program. He stayed up reading, catching up on housework, and completing a redo of his home office file system. Matt's new behavior increased what we call "sleep drive"—our bodies' hunger for healthy sleep. Within days Matt was asleep well before his usual 1 a.m. nodding off time. We then had him start going to bed at midnight, leaving all other parts of the program in place. When he was falling asleep before 12:30 we moved bedtime up to 11:30. Within a matter of weeks Matt was again going to bed at 10 p.m. but now was asleep within fifteen or twenty minutes. He also began getting out of bed earlier in the morning and feeling, for the first time in twenty years, rested, energetic, and ready to start his day.

EXPERIMENT XXV

ᔕ Restricting the Sandman

Step One: Calculate your actual "nodding off" time in the night or early morning.

Step Two: Add thirty minutes to this time and make this number your new bedtime.

Step Three: Set an alarm for a wake-up time that coincides if possible with the sun's appearance. When your alarm goes off, get out of bed for the day.

Step Four: Avoid naps or restrict them to no more than forty minutes before 4 p.m. each afternoon.

Step Five: When you are asleep in less than thirty minutes after your head hits the pillow, set a new bedtime thirty minutes prior to the old time.

Step Six: Continue this countdown until you've arrived at your desired schedule.

UNHELPFUL SLEEP BELIEFS

We've seen how our beliefs—helpful and unhelpful—often become self-fulfilling prophecies. Believing *Nothing will change* sets up thought patterns, negative feelings, and self-sabotaging behaviors that make this outcome more likely. When we've slept poorly for an extended time it is natural that our beliefs about this crucial part of life might take a hard turn for the worse.

Matt had many unhelpful sleep beliefs. These included beliefs we find again and again in our work with trauma patients struggling with insomnia. *My brain is just wired wrong. My past proves I'll never sleep well in the future. Awake now, I'll be unable to function tomorrow. If I sleep poorly one night I'll sleep poorly for several nights after. I can do nothing to sleep better.*

We taught Matt how to use the tools we call Hidden Wisdom, Price It, and New Deal to evaluate his commitment to these unhelpful sleep beliefs. He learned to identify the distortions in his thinking about sleep and to use the Get Real and Kernel of Truth tools to reset how he was viewing this part of life. Matt's beliefs began to shift. As he collected actual data showing his sleep was improving he began believing that he could, after all, create any relationship to sleep he wanted.

Interestingly Matt's daytime life, too, began to change. He returned to school and embarked on a new career path to become a physician's assistant. The last we heard from Matt he had made significant progress in his studies and was sleeping for the most part quite well. When he has an occasional night of poor sleep he sees it as an opportunity to use the tools he's mastered to *use* those wakeful hours instead of again being used *by* them.

You've now added a number of powerful CBT and sleep hygiene methods to your toolkit. Below we'll share some yoga therapy approaches to insomnia that research has demonstrated to be fast, safe, and effective sleep aids.

SLEEP LIKE A YOGI

Shabad Kriya is a yogic practice that two Harvard University studies have demonstrated to be effective for insomnia. Both studies found the practice of Shabad Kriya thirty minutes a day for eight weeks significantly improved sleep.[6] Subjects in both studies experienced improved sleep efficiency and more participants doing Shabad Kriya experienced normal sleep after eight weeks than participants in a control group receiving only sleep hygiene information.[7]

A recent study of Kundalini Yoga in a PTSD treatment program included Shabad Kriya. Participants in the program had significantly improved sleep as compared to those who were not in the program.[8] We teach Shabad Kriya in our Integrative Trauma Recovery Program. Outcome data on the program shows improvement in all PTSD symptoms, including insomnia. We've found significant improvements in total sleep scores, less sleep disturbance, less daytime dysfunction due to sleepiness, and better sleep quality following the program. At the three-month follow-up all these improvements have been maintained and sleep medication use has significantly decreased compared to the start of the program.[9]

Shabad Kriya may be practiced any time of day, the best time being just before going to bed. It is said that if it is practiced regularly, sleep will be deep and relaxed and the nerves will regenerate.[10]

This meditation uses the mantra Sat nam broken into four syllables—Sa Ta Na Ma—and recited silently. The "a" in each of these syllables sounds like "ah." The meanings of the syllables are as follows:

Sa: Infinity
Ta: Life (birth of form from Infinity)
Na: Death (or transformation)
Ma: Rebirth

Sa-Ta-Na-Ma describes the continuous cycle of life and creation.[11]

This meditation also uses the silent mantra *Wahe guru*. Though you will be projecting this mantra mentally, the "Wa" sounds like "wha," the "he" sounds like "hay," "gu" sounds like "good" without the "d," and "ru" rhymes with "true." The r sound is rolled slightly.

Wahe guru means "I am in ecstasy when I experience the indescribable wisdom." It expresses the indescribable experience of going from darkness to light (from ignorance to true understanding).[12]

Before doing this meditation, tune in by chanting "Ong namo guru dev namo" three times with your palms together at the center of your chest as described in chapter 7.

Posture

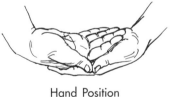

Hand Position

⁊ Shabad Kriya*

Posture: Sit in any comfortable posture with the spine straight. Place the hands in the lap, palms up with the right hand over the left. The thumbs are together and point forward.

Eyes: Focus the eyes on the tip of the nose, the eyelids nine-tenths closed.

Breath and mantra: Inhale in four equal parts, mentally vibrating the mantra Sa-Ta-Na-Ma. Hold the breath, vibrating the mantra four times for a total of sixteen beats. Exhale in two equal strokes, mentally projecting the mantra Wahe guru. Continue for fifteen to sixty-two minutes.

*Kundalini Yoga as taught by Yogi Bhajan® April 1, 1974

BREATHE YOURSELF ASLEEP

Long, deep breathing and left nostril breathing (described in chapter 7) may also help you relax and fall asleep. Both may be done either in bed or out (for example, while you're out of bed at night to avoid conditioned arousal). Left nostril breathing is associated with the ida energy channel and promotes relaxation, calm, sensitivity, and empathy. Research shows that left nostril breathing can also reduce sympathetic nervous system activity.[13] We have a natural nasal cycle that switches predominant airflow between nostrils every one and a half to four hours. The left-nostril dominance of this cycle can sometimes be induced simply by lying on your right side, which may help you fall asleep. Alternatively you may close your right nostril with your finger and breathe through the left nostril for several minutes.

As with all tools presented in this book, these yogic practices may or may not help you sleep. If one does help you, great! If it doesn't, set it aside and try another. Visit our website www.integrative-trauma-recovery .com to view a video of Shabad Kriya and review other resources in support of sound sleep.

9

The Road Forward

Human wellness is a daily phenomenon. The great life rhythms of land animals like ourselves—eating and fasting, sleeping and waking—follow a twenty-four-hour cycle that itself follows the sun. Chronobiology, the science that studies such rhythms, has mapped out many such cycles in the mammalian brain and body. These include not only observable behaviors but physiologic patterns as well—predictable variations in heart rate, body temperature, and cell metabolism—and cyclic changes in the level of hormones such as cortisol and melatonin. We humans are circadian creatures. Like the moon overhead and the ocean tides it governs, we live day-to-day on regular circuits of ebb and flow, departure and return.

When we're suffering from PTSD, dailiness can feel like a great foe. We come to dread a twenty-four-hour cycle of poor sleep, exhausted waking, and hour upon hour set out like mile markers on a lost highway of fear, anger, and loneliness. As days of such living become months and even years, we can feel we're living out a script invariant as that of an inmate serving a life sentence. Sunrise brings no joy, sunset no relief.

Yet when we're resolved to establish new habits of body and mind the brain's predisposition toward dailiness becomes a great ally. An activity that occurs each day, especially one that happens at about the same time, becomes incorporated into our physical and mental schemas at both conscious and subconscious levels. We begin to accept that activity as a given and its influence spreads far beyond the time spent doing it. Let's look at how this incorporation is taking place for one of our patients.

Pete grew up in a poor family that lived "on the wrong side of the tracks" in a large American city. He was physically small and one of a handful of white children at his grade school. Pete's schooldays followed a grindingly predictable circuit. Bullies would punch him on the walk to school, push him in front of oncoming traffic, take his lunch, and shout vicious things about Pete and his family. During recess Pete would be ridiculed, spat on, dunked headfirst in toilets, and have his clothing taken from him and thrown into trees. Pete was terrified of being murdered if he told his teachers what was happening so he kept his mouth shut. He tried telling his father, who flew into a rage, called Pete a "sissy," and told him to "stop whining like a little girl or I'll give you something real to whine about."

When Pete was in junior high his family moved to another city and the bullying ended. Yet without friends—or any idea about how to make them—Pete went on living a lonely, sad, and hopeless existence. Throughout high school Pete ate lunch standing in the pay phone booth pretending to be talking and laughing with someone on the other end of the line. By the time Pete came to us he was thirty-nine years old, still friendless, working in a dead-end job, and feeling suicidally depressed. From birth Pete's world had proven itself a hostile, cold place. He didn't see much point in continuing to live on such an alien planet.

At the same time Pete was aware that he'd never reached out for help, nor ever considered working on *himself*. We told Pete this made sense to us. Reaching out had regularly produced further suffering. Spending so much energy just putting one foot in front of the other, Pete had no strength left over with which to *work* on his life. He now felt he was standing at a crossroads. "It's do or die," Pete told us. "I'm almost forty. What I know for sure is I can't do this for another forty years."

Pete agreed to run an experiment in the cold, dark laboratory of his life. He committed to spending thirty minutes, six days per week, working with the tools laid out in this book. His lab book pages began filling with data as he worked with the tools of Hidden Wisdom, Price It, New Deal, and yoga kriya. We measured Pete's depression scores when we met each week and they began inching downward. For the first time in his life Pete realized that he was distorting his thinking. When he began disputing his distorted thoughts with the Get Real and Kernel of Truth tools, his depression scores came down more quickly. Pete began to consider the possibility that it wasn't the *world* that was his entire problem. How he was thinking and acting in the world were active ingredients in his suffering. Pete began connecting the dots, seeing more clearly how his distorted thinking and the behaviors that flowed from it "proved" his depressing beliefs about himself and others.

One way of understanding Pete's circadian reset is to see his thirty minutes of work on himself as his initiating a new habit. Most of what we do in any twenty-four hours is in fact habitual behavior. We get up at a certain time, which then triggers a predictable series of actions that carries us through our day. We don't make a conscious *decision* to brush our teeth, weighing the pros and cons of this choice against other alternatives. We simply find ourselves at the bathroom sink, staring sleepily into the mirror and brushing. When we resolve to reset our lives from PTSD we are deciding to create new habits of body, heart, and mind that will carry us through our days in new ways.

Each new year, one in two U.S. citizens resolves to change some habit. One third of them vow to lose weight. Others promise to quit smoking, start exercising, or find true love. Americans' track record on actually resetting such behaviors is not good. Fewer than 10 percent follow through and achieve their goals. Twenty-five percent will throw in the towel by January 8. What causes most people to stumble? More than anything else, the problem is misunderstanding the role of will-power in initiating and maintaining new behavior. Let's look together at this important point.

A prevailing cultural myth views brute willpower as the active ingredient in aligning our behavior with desired outcomes. Think of the maxims *Just say no! Just do it!* This myth considers *force of will* a muscle one develops to take oneself in hand and move toward one's goals. Often this prescription takes on moral overtones: "good" people act in accord with their stated goals and values. Such people "resist temptation" to fall into "vices" like inactivity, overeating, smoking cigarettes, and so forth.

There are two problems with this view. The first is that research data does not support it. Research shows that "effortful inhibition of impulses"—psychology's description of "resisting temptation"—is *negatively* correlated with self-control and goal achievement.[1] Highly successful people engage in far less effortful inhibition than do others. Rather than *effortfully* resisting, high achievers are carried *effortlessly* forward by force not of will but of habit. Habitual behavior carries them through their days like current on a river. They "just find themselves" brushing their teeth, exercising, eating well, working in productive ways, and so on.

The second problem with the force-of-will solution is that it sets us up in a power struggle with ourselves. A colleague refers to this as the "slave-driver dilemma." We pick up a stick to drive ourselves in some direction we think we "should" go. But as our colleague notes, "The natural thing for a slave to do is to revolt!" So slave driving actually sets us up for failure. Slave driving might get us a step or two down the road, but as is the case with 90 percent of New Year resolutionists, this approach soon backfires. When it does we resume smoking, stop exercising, return to our familiar habits, and now have the new problem of feeling discouraged, guilty, and bad about ourselves.

We helped Pete opt for force of *habit,* not of *will,* by setting things up as follows:

1. We had him select an amount of time each day he would very likely be able and willing to spend doing CBT and yoga homework. We urged him to set the bar low so as to increase the chances he would succeed in meeting his goal. We also wanted to make sure that twenty-four hours would not pass without Pete showing his brain that he was approaching his life in a new way. Pete selected thirty minutes and chose to set his alarm earlier in the morning to give himself this extra time.

2. We had Pete focus on the carrots, not the stick, in this new picture. We didn't want Pete driving himself with a stick—calling himself names, threatening himself, or sentencing himself to a lifetime of misery if he didn't do this work. Instead we encouraged him to look forward to receiving the benefits of his new behavior: feeling good, having friends, creating each day a bit more of a life worth living.

Pete found that while he only worked on himself thirty minutes each day, the rest of his waking hours began feeling different. When his breathing grew tight he noticed it and returned to the abdominal breathing he was practicing. When a "should" statement offered to plunge him into rage or self-loathing he realized he had a choice in the matter. He began looking forward to his practice time each day the way he looked forward to coffee in the morning and relaxing after work. Pete's recovery work started to become, like these other activities, habitual—a "given" part of his circadian existence. Thirty minutes of practice provided a little island of sanity he could plant at least one foot on at other times throughout his day. As the weeks passed Pete's depression scores continued down and he began experimenting with such new behaviors as going out with colleagues after work and registering with an online dating site.

Then something surprising happened. We were out of our offices for three weeks and when we again met with Pete his depression scores were as high as when we first started working together. We asked Pete if something terrible had happened while we were gone and he said no. His daily life looked pretty much as it had during the months he was feeling better—with one exception. Pete had stopped putting in his thirty minutes of work on himself six days per week. We asked Pete why he'd stopped his yoga and CBT practice and he said he figured he didn't need them anymore. Pete was now telling himself that CBT and yoga were not going to help him and that antidepressant medication was his only remaining option.

Pete was experiencing a full-blown relapse! We'd mentioned this possibility to him early in our work together. We told Pete that very often—in fact almost always—just as we begin to feel that we're finally out of the woods with PTSD, that we'll never again have to suffer those painful feelings and physical sensations, we wake one morning and they all come flooding back. Or something in our environment triggers us and we are plunged back into the old ways of thinking, feeling, and acting. Relapse often strikes when we've stopped working on recovery, telling ourselves as Pete did that we can now afford simply to coast along. Relapse feels even worse than our original suffering. We tell ourselves relapse "proves" that we're hopeless cases, that we "only thought" we'd gotten better, and that any further efforts in the directions we've been working would be pointless.

We empathized with Pete, expressed our sadness about his relapse, and gave our blessing to his looking in other directions for relief. At this point something interesting happened. Pete began arguing *against* his relapse thinking, saying that what had helped him so much the first time *might* again help him if he were willing to pick up these same tools and go back to daily work on his life. We agreed this seemed within the realm of possibility and noticed we now had a hypothesis that Pete could prove or disprove.

Pete decided to conduct a one-week experiment that involved his again putting in thirty minutes each day using the tools that had helped him in the past. When he returned the next week Pete's depression scores were lower than we'd ever seen them. The tools that had helped him in the past indeed helped again in exactly the same ways. Furthermore, crushing his relapse proved to Pete that he truly was the master of his emotional destiny. While outside events or letting up on his daily practice again presented Pete with emotional challenges he now felt 100 percent confident that he could address his distorted thinking and reset his mood and life course in any direction he wanted.

Something else happened that week. While cutting an apple at his kitchen counter Pete felt something new. Something he'd not felt before and so had no word to describe. As we listened to Pete we had a hunch what this emotion was, but we waited for him to voice it. Finally Pete hazarded a guess. "Maybe," he told us haltingly, "I felt happy." In the months, now years, since that day Pete has continued working on himself six days out of seven. It's no surprise that single moment of happiness has multiplied many times over and is now the emotional climate of Pete's life. He has a small circle of close friends, works at a new and rewarding job, and is keeping company with a wonderful woman Pete hopes will be his life partner.

Pete's experience is far from unique. Many research studies have shown the more people work on themselves, the more they improve. A large study that reviewed twenty-seven individual studies on CBT homework showed that participants who did more homework experienced more improvement.[2] Similar results have been discovered for yoga and meditation. A large study of more than one thousand yoga practitioners showed that greater frequency of yoga practice outside class correlated with greater well-being, better sleep, and less fatigue.[3] A study on mindfulness meditation that included a yoga component showed the amount of practice was directly related to decreases in stress and increases in psychological well-being.[4]

The benefits of regular practice extend far beyond improvements in mood and sleep. Regular yoga practice has been found to improve immune function.[5] Researchers have also observed that the number of years of yoga practice correlated to a protective effect on age-related loss of grey matter in the brain.[6] Two studies have been done specifically addressing yoga practice for PTSD. In a follow-up PTSD study, women who continued to practice yoga for one and a half years had fewer symptoms and were less likely to be diagnosable with PTSD.[7] Participants in a Kundalini Yoga as taught by Yogi Bhajan program for PTSD considered home practice "critical" to the program's success. Respondents expressed that "while initially a challenge to discipline oneself, the consistency, structure, and routine of having a self-healing practice that could be done anytime were vital to feelings of self-improvement and well-being."[8]

CAN DO

"Self-efficacy," a term coined by Stanford psychologist and former president of the American Psychological Association Albert Bandura, describes belief in one's ability to complete tasks and reach goals. Bandura notes that changing old habits and acquiring new ones involves two expectations. One, we anticipate new behavior producing new effects in our lives. Two, we expect that we will actually carry out and sustain the new behavior.[9] Yet the notion of self-efficacy is much older than modern psychology. Nearly two thousand years ago the Indian sage Patanjali wrote in his *Yoga Sutra* that faith and energy are the first steps in reaching the "supraconscious ecstasy" that is the goal of yoga.[10] Patanjali, too, speaks to the concept of self-efficacy: a *belief* we can achieve our goals produces the *motivation* to do so.

Self-efficacy is often examined in research studies. In one study breast-cancer survivors with greater self-efficacy were more likely to attend yoga classes.[11] And because self-efficacy drives behaviors associated with better treatment outcomes, researchers have been looking at ways to develop and increase this human quality. Both CBT and yoga have been shown to be mechanisms that do exactly that.[12] Pauri Kriya, presented below, was found to increase self-efficacy in HIV-positive patients.[13] Such research suggests we can create positive-feedback loops in our lives. Practicing yoga we increase self-efficacy—which in turn supports yoga practice. This is exactly what happens with the Motivator tool: our behavior creates willingness to continue the new behavior. As we reap the rewards of this virtuous cycle—greater happiness, self-worth, better sleep, and so on—the new behavior becomes encoded in the brain as a self-reinforcing part of our habitual repertoire.

As Bandura noted, in concert with all of the above, one additional thing happens: we change our beliefs about ourselves. Old self-sabotaging beliefs like *Things will never get better, I can't do anything right, There's no point in trying* give way to new, life-promoting beliefs in our capacity to create lives worth living. We've seen how belief is the ground from which all our thinking arises. Life-promoting beliefs produce new thought patterns, feelings, and habitual behavior that will increasingly carry us forward like current on a river toward all the destinations we would most like to reach. "Less and less do you need to force things," the *Tao Te Ching,* a classic Chinese text of philosophical guidance, tells us. "When nothing is [forcefully] done, nothing is left undone."[14]

Let's look now at our final trauma recovery tool, Pauri Kriya. As it helped HIV-positive patients enhance their experience of self-efficacy it might well help you do the same.

ȣ Pauri Kriya*

Like Shabad Kriya presented in the previous chapter, Pauri Kriya uses the mantra Sat nam broken into four syllables, Sa-Ta-Na-Ma, recited both silently and aloud. Please see chapter 8, page 141, for the explanation of how this mantra sounds and its meaning.

Begin by tuning in, as we did with our other Kundalini Yoga meditations. This is done by chanting "Ong namo guru dev namo" three times with your palms together at the center of your chest as described in chapter 7 (see pages 120–21). You may also see this meditation described and demonstrated on a video at www.integrative-trauma-recovery.com.

---

*Kundalini Yoga as taught by Yogi Bhajan®

Posture

Sit comfortably with your spine aligned. Rest your hands on your knees, palms facing up, with elbows straight. Close your eyes.

Inhale by dividing the breath into eight equal, separate parts, like sniffs. On the first segment of the eight parts, silently repeat the sound of Sa, on the second silently repeat Ta, on the third repeat Na, on the fourth repeat Ma. Silently repeat Sa on the fifth, Ta on the sixth, Na on the seventh, and Ma on the eighth part of the eight-part inhalation.

Finger Positions, SA

Finger Positions, TA

Finger Positions, NA

Finger Positions, MA

While you breathe and silently repeat the sounds, move the fingers of each hand in the following sequence: On Sa press the tips of the index finger and thumb firmly together, on Ta press the middle finger and thumb tips, on Na press the ring finger and thumb tips, and on Ma press the little finger and thumb tips together.

To exhale the breath, recite aloud, Sa-Ta-Na-Ma Sa-Ta-Na-Ma in a monotone. Coordinate the pressing of the thumb tips to the fingers with the corresponding sounds, just as you did during the silent eight-part inhalation.

Continue this sequence for eleven to sixty-two minutes. If you notice your mind wandering, simply return your attention to the breath, sound, and finger sequence of the meditation.

At the end of the meditation, inhale in one long breath, retain your breath briefly, and exhale in one long breath. Relax your posture and open your eyes.

THE ROAD FORWARD

The Old English term *foreweard* is the root of our word "forward." *Foreweard* carried such meanings as "inclined to the front," "early," and "former." We very much like these connotations. When we're living *out in front* of our lives we're not hiding behind anything. When we're *early* in our living we're not overthinking things or involved with security operations that emerge downstream of our negative thoughts. As a result we're more spontaneous, open, ourselves. We might conceptualize trauma recovery as return to our *former,* pre-trauma selves.

At the beginning of this book we noted Buddhism's first noble truth: "Life is suffering." We've also noted that all the great world paths give us their version of the declaration "Happiness is our birthright." Such statements do not contradict each other: they are, rather, like two feet walking. Every hour of every day brings its form of suffering. Something doesn't go our way. Someone says an unkind word. Our physical comfort or wellness is threatened in ways great or small. Yet whatever the circumstances of our lives we have the possibility of using these to experience and deepen the happiness that is at the center of human living and dying. We hope that this book has provided you with new tools to do exactly that.

We can consider cognition and physicality the walls, floor, and roof of our first home. What we think and how we carry ourselves through our days and nights provide the primary structure in which we live. Any structures farther away than this—our physical houses, nation states, and so on—are perhaps less influential in regard to our happiness than this first. People with very little outside structure regularly live profoundly happy, meaningful lives. And people who seem from the outside to "have it all" are sometimes so unhappy they kill themselves. It seems the Greek Stoics had it right: it's not what befalls us but what we tell ourselves that determines the quality of our human experience.

Any road forward is no other than the ground beneath our feet. We are, in fact, always already on the path. As you walk this road with all your fellow beings, we invite you to share your experiences along the way. Visit our website www.integrative-trauma-recovery.com and receive updated information about trauma recovery, find the dates of upcoming Integrative Trauma Recovery Program retreats, and be inspired to keep your own feet firmly on the road forward. We look forward to continuing to walk this path with you.

Notes

I. ROOTS OF THE PROBLEM

1. Aitken, *The Morning Star*, 6.
2. Bhajan, "Yogi Bhajan Lecture: Happiness," www.3ho.org/yogi-bhajan/yogi
-bhajan-lectures/yogi-bhajan-lecture-happiness.

2. EMBODIED STRESS

1. Flückiger-Hawker, *Urnamma of Ur in Sumerian Literary Tradition*, 19–20.
2. Shin, Rauch, and Pitman, "Amygdala, Medial Prefrontal Cortex, and Hippocampal Function in PTSD," 67–79.
3. Dyck et al., "Cognitive versus Automatic Mechanisms of Mood Induction Differentially Activate Left and Right Amygdala," 2503–13.
4. Pissiota et al., "Neurofunctional Correlates of Posttraumatic Stress Disorder," 68–75.
5. Kalyani et al., "Neurohemodynamic Correlates of 'Om' Chanting," 3–6.
6. Desbordes et al., "Effects of Mindful-Attention and Compassion Meditation Training on Amygdala Response," 292.
7. Felmingham et al., "Changes in Anterior Cingulate and Amygdala after Cognitive Behavior Therapy of Posttraumatic Stress Disorder," 127–29.
8. Shin, Rauch, and Pitman, "Amygdala, Medial Prefrontal Cortex," 67–79.
9. Gilbertson et al., "Smaller Hippocampal Volume Predicts Pathologic Vulnerability to Psychological Trauma," 1242–47.

10. Apfel et al., "Hippocampal Volume Differences in Gulf War Veterans," 541–48.

11. Gotink et al., "8-Week Mindfulness-Based Stress Reduction Induces Brain Changes," 32–41.

12. Hariprasad et al., "Yoga Increases the Volume of the Hippocampus," S394–96.

13. Szabó, Kelemen, and Kéri, "Changes in FKBP5 Expression and Memory Functions during Cognitive-Behavioral Therapy in Posttraumatic Stress Disorder," 116–20.

14. Fragkaki, Thomaes, and Sijbrandij, "Posttraumatic Stress Disorder Under Ongoing Threat," 30915.

15. O'Doherty et al., "A Systematic Review and Meta-Analysis of Magnetic Resonance Imaging Measurement of Structural Volumes in Posttraumatic Stress Disorder," 1–33.

16. Shin et al., "An FMRI Study of Anterior Cingulate Function in Posttraumatic Stress Disorder," 932–42.

17. Karl et al., "A Meta-Analysis of Structural Brain Abnormalities in PTSD," 1004–31.

18. Kasai et al., "Evidence for Acquired Pregenual Anterior Cingulate Gray Matter Loss from a Twin Study," 550–56.

19. Grant et al., "Cortical Thickness and Pain Sensitivity in Zen Meditators," 43–53.

20. Hölzel et al., "Differential Engagement of Anterior Cingulate and Adjacent Medial Frontal Cortex in Adept Meditators and Non-Meditators," 16–21.

21. Felmingham et al., "Changes in Anterior Cingulate and Amygdala after Cognitive Behavior Therapy of Posttraumatic Stress Disorder," 127–29.

22. Meyerhoff et al., "Cortical Gamma-Aminobutyric Acid and Glutamate in Posttraumatic Stress Disorder," 893–900; and Trousselard et al., "Is Plasma GABA Level a Biomarker of Post-Traumatic Stress Disorder (PTSD) Severity?" 273–79.

23. Streeter et al., "Effects of Yoga versus Walking on Mood, Anxiety, and Brain GABA Levels," 1145–52.

24. Streeter et al., "Yoga Asana Sessions Increase Brain GABA Levels," 419–26.

25. Chalmers et al., "Anxiety Disorders Are Associated with Reduced Heart Rate Variability," 80.

26. Minassian et al., "Association of Predeployment Heart Rate Variability with Risk of Postdeployment Posttraumatic Stress Disorder," 979–86.

27. Markil et al., "Yoga Nidra Relaxation Increases Heart Rate Variability," 953–58; and Santaella et al., "Yoga Respiratory Training Improves Respiratory Function and Cardiac Sympathovagal Balance," e000085.

28. Nishith et al., "Effect of Cognitive Behavioral Therapy on Heart Rate Variability," 247–50.

29. McEwen, "Protective and Damaging Effects of Stress Mediators," 171–79.

30. Glover, Stuber, and Poland, "Allostatic Load in Women with and without PTSD Symptoms," 191–203.

31. Carroll et al., "Improved Sleep Quality in Older Adults with Insomnia Reduces Biomarkers of Disease Risk," 184–92.

32. Pascoe and Bauer, "A Systematic Review of Randomized Control Trials on the Effects of Yoga on Stress Measures and Mood," 270–82.

33. Szabó, Kelemen, and Kéri, "Changes in FKBP5 Expression," 116–20.

34. Passos et al., "Inflammatory Markers in Post-Traumatic Stress Disorder," 1002–12; and Wang and Young, "PTSD, a Disorder with an Immunological Component," 219.

35. Kiecolt-Glaser et al., "Adiponectin, Leptin, and Yoga Practice," 809–13; Bower and Irwin, "Mind-Body Therapies and Control of Inflammatory Biology," 1–11; and Rajbhoj et al., "Effect of Yoga Module on Pro-Inflammatory and Anti-Inflammatory Cytokines," CC01–CC05.

36. Moreira et al., "The Effect of Proinflammatory Cytokines in Cognitive Behavioral Therapy," 143–46.

37. Black et al., "Yogic Meditation Reverses NF-KappaB and IRF-Related Transcriptome Dynamics in Leukocytes," 348–55.

38. Bower et al., "Yoga Reduces Inflammatory Signaling in Fatigued Breast Cancer Survivors," 20–29.

39. Antoni et al., "Cognitive-Behavioral Stress Management Reverses Anxiety-Related Leukocyte Transcriptional Dynamics," 366–72.

40. Lindqvist et al., "Psychiatric Disorders and Leukocyte Telomere Length," 333–64.

41. Krishna et al., "Association of Leukocyte Telomere Length with Oxidative Stress in Yoga Practitioners," CC01–CC03.

42. Jindani, Turner, and Khalsa, "A Yoga Intervention for Posttraumatic Stress," 351746.

43. Jindani and Khalsa, "A Yoga Intervention Program for Patients Suffering from Symptoms of Posttraumatic Stress Disorder," 401–8.

44. Van der Kolk et al., "Yoga as an Adjunctive Treatment for Posttraumatic Stress Disorder," e559–e565; Johnston et al., "Yoga for Military Service Personnel with PTSD," 555–62; Quiñones et al., "Efficacy of a Satyananda Yoga Intervention for Reintegrating Adults Diagnosed with Posttraumatic Stress Disorder," 89–99; and Staples, Hamilton, and Uddo, "A Yoga Program for the Symptoms of Posttraumatic Stress Disorder," 854–60.

45. Bormann et al., "Meditation-Based Mantram Intervention for Veterans with Posttraumatic Stress Disorder," 259–67; Kearney et al., "Association of Participation in a Mindfulness Program with Measures of PTSD, Depression, and Quality of Life," 101–16; and Seppälä et al., "Breathing-Based Meditation Decreases Posttraumatic Stress Disorder Symptoms," 397–405.

46. Staples, Mintie, and Khalsa, "Evaluation of a Combined Yoga and Cognitive Behavioral Therapy Program for Posttraumatic Stress Disorder," A94.

5. REWIRE YOUR BRAIN

1. Ellis, "New Approaches to Psychotherapy Techniques," 207–60.

6. BELIEF: THE HEART OF THE MATTER

1. Ellis and Lang, *How to Keep People from Pushing Your Buttons,* 79–80.

2. Wittgenstein, *On Certainty,* 47.

7. YOGA: EMBODIED WELLNESS

1. Prabhavananda and Isherwood, *How to Know God,* 15–94.

2. Sovik and Bhavanani, *The Principles and Practice of Yoga in Healthcare,* 17–29.

3. Bhajan, "Breath (Pranayam)," 92.

4. Spicuzza et al., "Yoga and Chemoreflex Response to Hypoxia and Hypercapnia," 1495–96.

5. 3HO Happy Healthy Holy Organization, "Self-Care Breath Kriya," www.3ho.org/3ho-lifestyle/healthy-happy-holy-lifestyle/happy/self-care-breath-kriya; and Bhajan, "Breath (Pranayam)," 97.

6. S. S. K. Khalsa, "Supporting People with Posttraumatic Stress Disorder (PTSD) through Kundalini Yoga," 30.

7. S. B. S. Khalsa, "Treatment of Chronic Insomnia With Yoga," 269–78.

8. Bhajan, "Kriya in Kundalini Yoga," 105.

9. Bhajan, "Kriya in Kundalini Yoga," 105.

10. Khalsa and Gould, "Finding the Right Style of Yoga for You," chap. 5.

11. Bhajan, "Yogic Anatomy," 176.

12. Staples, Mintie, and Khalsa, "Evaluation of a Combined Yoga and Cognitive Behavioral Therapy Program for Posttraumatic Stress Disorder," A94; Jindani, Turner, and Khalsa, "A Yoga Intervention for Posttraumatic Stress," 351746; and Jindani and Khalsa, "A Yoga Intervention Program for Patients Suffering from Symptoms of Posttraumatic Stress Disorder," 401–8.

13. Bhajan, "Sound and Mantra," 66.

14. Bhajan, "Kriya in Kundalini Yoga," 100.

15. Bhajan, "The Mind and Meditation," 136.

16. S. S. K. Khalsa, "Supporting People with Posttraumatic Stress Disorder (PTSD) through Kundalini Yoga," 25.

17. 3HO Happy Healthy Holy Organization, "Covering the Head," www.3ho .org/3ho-lifestyle/daily-routine/covering-head.

18. Bhajan, "Yogic Anatomy," 178.

19. S. S. K. Khalsa, "Supporting People with Posttraumatic Stress Disorder," 28.

20. Staples, Mintie, and Khalsa, "Evaluation of a Combined Yoga and Cognitive Behavioral Therapy Program for Posttraumatic Stress Disorder," A94.

21. H. K. Khalsa, *Self-Knowledge,* 41–42.

22. S. S. K. Khalsa, "Supporting People with Posttraumatic Stress Disorder," 31.

8. SLEEP WELL

1. Cribbet et al., "Cellular Aging and Restorative Processes," 65–70.

2. Xie et al., "Sleep Drives Metabolite Clearance from the Adult Brain," 373–77.

3. Gross et al., "Mindfulness-Based Stress Reduction versus Pharmacotherapy for Chronic Primary Insomnia," 76–87.

4. Mitchell et al., "Comparative Effectiveness of Cognitive Behavioral Therapy for Insomnia," 40.

5. Ho, Chan, and Tang, "Cognitive-Behavioral Therapy for Sleep Disturbances in Treating Posttraumatic Stress Disorder Symptoms," 90–102; Jindani, Turner, and Khalsa, "A Yoga Intervention for Posttraumatic Stress,"

351746; and Staples, Mintie, and Khalsa, "Evaluation of a Combined Yoga and Cognitive Behavioral Therapy Program for Posttraumatic Stress Disorder," A94.

6. S. B. S. Khalsa, "Treatment of Chronic Insomnia with Yoga," 269–78, and, "A Randomized Controlled Trial of a Yoga Treatment for Chronic Insomnia," 179.

7. S. B. S. Khalsa, "Yoga Treatment for Chronic Insomnia," 179.

8. Jindani, Turner, and Khalsa, "A Yoga Intervention for Posttraumatic Stress," 351746.

9. Staples, Mintie, and Khalsa, "Evaluation of a Combined Yoga and Cognitive Behavioral Therapy Program," A94.

10. Bhajan, *Kundalini Meditation Manual for Intermediate Students,* 50.

11. Bhajan, "Sound and Mantra," 87.

12. Bhajan, "Sound and Mantra," 87.

13. Telles, Nagarathna, and Nagendra, "Breathing through a Particular Nostril Can Alter Metabolism and Autonomic Activities," 133–37.

9. THE ROAD FORWARD

1. Galla and Duckworth, "More Than Resisting Temptation," 508–25.

2. Kazantzis, Dean, and Ronan, "Homework Assignments in Cognitive Behavioral Therapy," 189–202.

3. Ross et al., "Frequency of Yoga Practice Predicts Health," 983258.

4. Carmody and Baer, "Relationships between Mindfulness Practice and Levels of Mindfulness, Medical and Psychological Symptoms, and Well-Being," 23–33.

5. Kiecolt-Glaser et al., "Adiponectin, Leptin, and Yoga Practice," 809–13.

6. Villemure et al., "Neuroprotective Effects of Yoga Practice," 281.

7. Rhodes, Spinazzola, and van der Kolk, "Yoga for Adult Women with Chronic PTSD," 189–96.

8. Jindani and Khalsa, "A Yoga Intervention Program for Patients Suffering from Symptoms of Posttraumatic Stress Disorder," 405.

9. Strecher et al., "The Role of Self-Efficacy in Achieving Health Behavior Change," 73–92.

10. Feuerstein, "The History and Literature of Patanjali Yoga," 218.

11. Cadmus-Bertram et al., "Predictors of Adherence to a 26-Week Viniyoga Intervention," 751–58.

12. Gallagher et al., "Mechanisms of Change in Cognitive Behavioral Therapy for Panic Disorder," 767–77; and Bonura and Tenenbaum, "Effects of Yoga on Psychological Health in Older Adults," 1334–41.

13. S. S. K. Khalsa, "The Effects of Two Types of Meditation Techniques on Self-Efficacy Beliefs," Ph.D. diss.

14. Mitchell, trans., *Tao Te Ching*, verse 48.

Bibliography

3HO Happy Healthy Holy Organization. "Covering the Head," accessed October 29, 2016: www.3ho.org/3ho-lifestyle/daily-routine/covering-head.

3HO Happy Healthy Holy Organization. "Self-Care Breath Kriya," accessed October 29, 2016: www.3ho.org/3ho-lifestyle/healthy-happy-holy-lifestyle /happy/self-care-breath-kriya.

Aitken, Robert, *The Morning Star: New and Selected Zen Writings*. Berkeley, Calif.: Counterpoint, 2003.

Antoni, Micheal H., Susan K. Lutgendorf, Bonnie Blomberg, Charles S. Carver, Suzanne Lechner, Alain Diaz, Jamie Stagl, Jesusa M. G. Arevalo, and Steven W. Cole. "Cognitive-Behavioral Stress Management Reverses Anxiety-Related Leukocyte Transcriptional Dynamics." *Biological Psychiatry* 71, no. 4 (February 2012): 366–72. doi:10.1016/j.biopsych.2011.10.007.

Apfel, Brigitte A., Jessica Ross, Jennifer Hlavin, Dieter J. Meyerhoff, Thomas J. Metzler, Charles R. Marmar, Michael W. Weiner, Norbert Schuff, and Thomas C. Neylan. "Hippocampal Volume Differences in Gulf War Veterans with Current versus Lifetime Posttraumatic Stress Disorder Symptoms." *Biological Psychiatry* 69, no. 6 (March 2011): 541–48. doi:10.1016 /j.biopsych.2010.09.044.

Bhajan, Yogi, "Breath (Pranayam)." Chap. 8 in *The Aquarian Teacher,* edited by Khalsa Guru Raj Kaur, Gurucharan Singh Khalsa, Shakti Parwha Kaur Khalsa, John Ricker, and Guruka Singh Khalsa. Santa Cruz, N.Mex.: Kundalini Research Institute, 2003.

———. "Kriya in Kundalini Yoga: Asana, Mudra, and Bhanda." Chap. 9 in *The Aquarian Teacher,* edited by Khalsa Guru Raj Kaur, Gurucharan Singh Khalsa, Shakti Parwha Kaur Khalsa, John Ricker, and Guruka Singh Khalsa. Santa Cruz, N.Mex.: Kundalini Research Institute, 2003.

———. *Kundalini Meditation Manual for Intermediate Students.* Santa Cruz, N.Mex.: Kundalini Research Institute, 1979.

———. "Sound and Mantra." Chap. 7 in *The Aquarian Teacher,* edited by Khalsa Guru Raj Kaur, Gurucharan Singh Khalsa, Shakti Parwha Kaur Khalsa, John Ricker, and Guruka Singh Khalsa. Santa Cruz, N.Mex.: Kundalini Research Institute, 2003.

———. "The Mind and Meditation." Chap. 11 in *The Aquarian Teacher,* edited by Khalsa Guru Raj Kaur, Gurucharan Singh Khalsa, Shakti Parwha Kaur Khalsa, John Ricker, and Guruka Singh Khalsa. Santa Cruz, N.Mex.: Kundalini Research Institute, 2003.

———. "Yogic Anatomy: Prana, Vayus, Nadis, the Kundalini and the Navel Point." Chap. 14 in *The Aquarian Teacher,* edited by Khalsa Guru Raj Kaur, Gurucharan Singh Khalsa, Shakti Parwha Kaur Khalsa, John Ricker, and Guruka Singh Khalsa. Santa Cruz, N.Mex.: Kundalini Research Institute, 2003.

———. "Yogi Bhajan Lecture: Happiness" (Los Angeles, 1989). www.3ho.org/yogi-bhajan/yogi-bhajan-lectures/yogi-bhajan-lecture-happiness.

Black, David S., Steve Cole, Michael R. Irwin, Elizabeth Breen, Natalie M. St Cyr, Nora Nazarian, Dharma S. Khalsa, and Helen Lavretsky. "Yogic Meditation Reverses NF-KappaB and IRF-Related Transcriptome Dynamics in Leukocytes of Family Dementia Caregivers in a Randomized Controlled Trial." *Psychoneuroendocrinology* 38, no. 3 (March 2013): 348–55. doi:10.1016/j.psyneuen.2012.06.011.

Bonura, Kimberlee Bethany, and Gershon Tenenbaum. "Effects of Yoga on Psychological Health in Older Adults." *Journal of Physical Activity and Health* 11, no. 7 (September 2014): 1334–41. doi:10.1123/jpah.2012–0365.

Bormann, Jill E., Steven E. Thorp, Julie L. Wetherell, Shahrokh Golshan, and Ariel J. Lang. "Meditation-Based Mantram Intervention for Veterans with Posttraumatic Stress Disorder: A Randomized Trial." *Psychological Trauma: Theory, Research, Practice, and Policy* 5, no. 3 (2013): 259–67. doi:10.1037/a0027522.

Bower, Julienne E., Gail Greendale, Alexandra D. Crosswell, Deborah Garet,

Beth Sternlieb, Patricia A. Ganz, Michael R. Irwin, et al. "Yoga Reduces Inflammatory Signaling in Fatigued Breast Cancer Survivors: A Randomized Controlled Trial." *Psychoneuroendocrinology* 43 (May 2014): 20–29. doi:10.1016/j.psyneuen.2014.01.019.

Bower, Julienne E., and Michael R. Irwin. "Mind-Body Therapies and Control of Inflammatory Biology: A Descriptive Review." *Brain Behavior and Immunity* 51 (January 2016): 1–11. doi:10.1016/j.bbi.2015.06.012.

Cadmus-Bertram, Lisa, Alyson J. Littman, Cornelia M. Ulrich, Rachael Stovall, Rachel M. Ceballos, Bonnie A. McGregor, Ching-Yun Wang, Jaya Ramaprasad, and Anne McTiernan. "Predictors of Adherence to a 26-Week Viniyoga Intervention among Post-Treatment Breast Cancer Survivors." *The Journal of Alternative and Complementary Medicine* 19, no. 9 (September 2013): 751–58. doi:10.1089/acm.2012.0118.

Carmody, James, and Ruth A. Baer. "Relationships between Mindfulness Practice and Levels of Mindfulness, Medical and Psychological Symptoms, and Well-Being in a Mindfulness-Based Stress-Reduction Program." *Journal of Behavioral Medicine* 31, no. 1 (February 2008): 23–33. doi:10.1007/s10865-007-9130-7.

Carroll, Judith E., Teresa E. Seeman, Richard Olmstead, Gerson Melendez, Ryan Sadakane, Richard Bootzin, Perry Nicassio, and Michael R. Irwin. "Improved Sleep Quality in Older Adults with Insomnia Reduces Biomarkers of Disease Risk: Pilot Results from a Randomized Controlled Comparative Efficacy Trial." *Psychoneuroendocrinology* 55 (May 2015): 184–92. doi:10.1016/j.psyneuen.2015.02.010.

Chalmers, John A., Daniel S. Quintana, Maree J. Ann Abbott, and Andrew H. Kemp. "Anxiety Disorders Are Associated with Reduced Heart Rate Variability: A Meta-Analysis." *Frontiers in Psychiatry* 5 (July 2014): 80. doi:10.3389/fpsyt.2014.00080.

Cribbet, Matthew R., McKenzie Carlisle, Richard M. Cawthon, Bert N. Uchino, Paula G. Williams, Timothy W. Smith, Heather E. Gunn, and Kathleen C. Light. "Cellular Aging and Restorative Processes: Subjective Sleep Quality and Duration Moderate the Association between Age and Telomere Length in a Sample of Middle-Aged and Older Adults." *Sleep* 37, no. 1 (January 2014): 65–70. doi:10.5665/sleep.3308.

Desbordes, Gaëlle, Lobsang T. Negi, Thaddeus W. W. Pace, B. Alan Wallace, Charles L. Raison, and Eric L. Schwartz. "Effects of Mindful-Attention and Compassion Meditation Training on Amygdala Response to Emotional Stimuli in an Ordinary, Non-Meditative State." *Frontiers in Human Neuroscience* 6 (November 2012): 292. doi:10.3389/fnhum.2012.00292.

Dyck, Miriam, James Loughead, Thilo Kellermann, Frank Boers, Ruben C. Gur, and Klaus Mathiak. "Cognitive versus Automatic Mechanisms of Mood Induction Differentially Activate Left and Right Amygdala." *Neuroimage* 54, no. 3 (February 2011): 2503–13. doi:10.1016/j.neuroimage.2010.10.013.

Ellis, Albert. "New Approaches to Psychotherapy Techniques." *Journal of Clinical Psychology* 11 (1955): 207–60. doi:10.1002/1097–4679(195507)11:3<207 ::AID-JCLP2270110302>3.0.CO;2–1.

Ellis, Albert, and Arthur Lang. *How to Keep People from Pushing Your Buttons*, New York: Citadel, 2003.

Felmingham, Kim, Andrew Kemp, Leanne Williams, Pritha Das, Gerard Hughes, Anthony Peduto, and Richard Bryant. "Changes in Anterior Cingulate and Amygdala after Cognitive Behavior Therapy of Posttraumatic Stress Disorder." *Psychological Science* 18, no. 2 (February 2007): 127–29. doi:10.1111/j.1467-9280.2007.01860.x.

Feuerstein, Georg. "The History and Literature of Patanjali-Yoga." Chap. 9 in *The Yoga Tradition: Its History, Literature, Philosophy, and Practice* (Yoga Sutra 1.20-1.21). Prescott, AZ: Hohm Press, 2001.

Flückiger-Hawker, Esther. *Urnamma of Ur in Sumerian Literary Tradition.* Fribourg, Switzerland: University Press, 1999.

Fragkaki, Iro, Kathleen Thomaes, and Marit Sijbrandij. "Posttraumatic Stress Disorder Under Ongoing Threat: A Review of Neurobiological and Neuroendocrine Findings." *European Journal of Psychotraumatology* 7 (August 2016): 30915. doi:10.3402/ejpt.v7.30915.

Galla, Brian M., and Angela L. Duckworth. "More Than Resisting Temptation: Beneficial Habits Mediate the Relationship between Self-Control and Positive Life Outcomes." *Journal of Personality and Social Psychology* 109, no. 3 (September 2015): 508–25. doi:10.1037/pspp0000026.

Gallagher, Matthew W., Laura A. Payne, Kamila S. White, Katherine M. Shear, Scott W. Woods, Jack M. Gorman, and David H. Barlow. "Mechanisms of Change in Cognitive Behavioral Therapy for Panic Disorder: the Unique Effects of Self-Efficacy and Anxiety Sensitivity." *Behavior Research and Therapy* 51, no. 11 (November 2013): 767–77. doi:10.1016 /j.brat.2013.09.001.

Gilbertson, Mark W., Martha E. Shenton, Aleksandra Ciszewski, Kiyoto Kasai, Natasha B. Lasko, Scott P. Orr, and Roger K. Pitman. "Smaller Hippocampal Volume Predicts Pathologic Vulnerability to Psychological Trauma." *Nature Neuroscience* 5, no. 11 (November 2002): 1242–47. doi:10.1038/nn958.

Glover, Dorie A., Margaret Stuber, and Russel E. Poland. "Allostatic Load in Women with and without PTSD Symptoms." *Psychiatry* 69, no. 3 (2006): 191–203. doi:10.1521/psyc.2006.69.3.191.

Gotink, Rinske A., Rozanna Meijboom, Meike W. Vernooij, Marion Smits, and M. G. Myriam Hunink. "8-Week Mindfulness-Based Stress Reduction Induces Brain Changes Similar to Traditional Long-Term Meditation Practice: A Systematic Review." *Brain and Cognition* 108 (October 2016): 32–41. doi:10.1016/j.bandc.2016.07.001.

Grant, Joshua A., Jérôme Courtemanche, Emma G. Duerden, Gary H. Duncan, and Pierre Rainville. "Cortical Thickness and Pain Sensitivity in Zen Meditators." *Emotion* 10, no. 1 (February 2010): 43–53. doi:10.1037/a0018334.

Gross, Cynthia R., Mary Jo Kreitzer, Maryanne Reilly-Spong, Melanie Wall, Nicole Y. Winbush, Robert Patterson, Mark Mahowald, and Michel Cramer-Bornemann. "Mindfulness-Based Stress Reduction versus Pharmacotherapy for Chronic Primary Insomnia: A Randomized Controlled Clinical Trial." *Explore (NY)* 7, no. 2 (March 2011): 76–87. doi:10.1016/j.explore.2010.12.003.

Hariprasad, V. R., S. Varambally, V. Shivakumar, S. V. Kalmady, G. Venkatasubramanian, and B. N. Gangadhar. "Yoga Increases the Volume of the Hippocampus in Elderly Subjects." *Indian Journal of Psychiatry* 55, no. Suppl 3 (July 2013): S394-S396. doi:10.4103/0019-5545.116309.

Ho, Fiona Yan-Yee, Christian S. Chan, and Kristen Nga-Sze Tang. "Cognitive-Behavioral Therapy for Sleep Disturbances in Treating Posttraumatic Stress Disorder Symptoms: A Meta-Analysis of Randomized Controlled Trials." *Clinical Psychology Review* 43 (February 2016): 90–102. doi:10.1016/j.cpr.2015.09.005.

Hölzel, Britta K., U lrich Ott, Hannes Hempel, Andrea Hackl, Katharina Wolf, Rudolf Stark, and Dieter Vaitl. "Differential Engagement of Anterior Cingulate and Adjacent Medial Frontal Cortex in Adept Meditators and Non-Meditators." *Neuroscience Letters* 421, no. 1 (June 2007): 16–21. doi:10.1016/j.neulet.2007.04.074.

Jindani, Farah, Nigel Turner, and Sat Bir S. Khalsa. "A Yoga Intervention for Posttraumatic Stress: A Preliminary Randomized Control Trial." *Evidence-Based Complementary and Alternative Medicine* 2015 (2015): 351746. doi:10.1155/2015/351746.

Jindani, Farah A., and G. F. S. Khalsa. "A Yoga Intervention Program for Patients Suffering from Symptoms of Posttraumatic Stress Disorder: A Qualitative Descriptive Study." *The Journal of Alternative and Complementary Medicine* 21, no. 7 (July 2015): 401–8. doi:10.1089/acm.2014.0262.

Johnston, Jennifer M., Takuya Minami, Deborah Greenwald, Chieh Li, Kristen Reinhardt, and Sat Bir Singh Khalsa. "Yoga for Military Service Personnel with PTSD: A Single-Arm Study." *Psychological Trauma: Theory, Research, Practice and Policy* 7, no. 6 (November 2015): 555–62. doi:10.1037/tra0000051.

Kalyani, Bangalore G., Ganesan Venkatasubramanian, Rashmi Arasappa, Naren P. Rao, Sunil V. Kalmady, Rishikesh V. Behere, Hariprasad Rao, Mandapati K. Vasudev, and Bangalore N. Gangadhar. "Neurohemodynamic Correlates of 'Om' Chanting: A Pilot Functional Magnetic Resonance Imaging Study." *International Journal of Yoga* 4, no. 1 (January 2011): 3–6. doi:10.4103/0973-6131.78171.

Karl, Anke, Michael Schaefer, Loretta S. Malta, Denise Dörfel, Nicholas Rohleder, and Annett Werner. "A Meta-Analysis of Structural Brain Abnormalities in PTSD." *Neuroscience and Biobehavioral Reviews* 30, no. 7 (2006): 1004–31. doi:10.1016/j.neubiorev.2006.03.004.

Kasai, Kiyoto, Hinenorni Yamasue, Mark W. Gilbertson, Martha E. Shenton, Scott L. Rauch, and Roger K. Pitman. "Evidence for Acquired Pregenual Anterior Cingulate Gray Matter Loss from a Twin Study of Combat-Related Posttraumatic Stress Disorder." *Biological Psychiatry* 63, no. 6 (March 2008): 550–56. doi:10.1016/j.biopsych.2007.06.022.

Kazantzis, Nikoloas, Frank P. Dean, and Kevin R. Ronan. "Homework Assignments in Cognitive Behavioral Therapy: A Meta Analysis." *Clinical Psychology: Science and Practice* 7, no. 2 (2000): 189–202. doi:10.1093/clipsy.7.2.189.

Kearney, David J., Kelly McDermott, Carol Malte, Michelle Martinez, and Tracy L. Simpson. "Association of Participation in a Mindfulness Program with Measures of PTSD, Depression, and Quality of Life in a Veteran Sample." *Journal of Clinical Psychology* 68, no. 1 (January 2012): 101–16. doi:10.1002/jclp.20853.

Khalsa, Harijot Kaur, *Self-Knowledge: Kundalini Yoga as Taught by Yogi Bhajan*. Espanola, N.Mex.: Ravitej Singh Khalsa, 1995.

Khalsa, Sat Bir Singh. "Treatment of Chronic Insomnia with Yoga: A Preliminary Study with Sleep-Wake Diaries." *Applied Psychophysiology and Biofeedback* 29, no. 4 (December 2004): 269–78. doi:10.1007/s10484-004-0387-0.

———. "A Randomized Controlled Trial of a Yoga Treatment for Chronic Insomnia." *Applied Psychophysiology and Biofeedback* 35 (2010): 179.

Khalsa, Sat Bir Singh, and Jodie Gould. "Finding the Right Style of Yoga for You." Chap. 5 in *Your Brain on Yoga*. New York: RosettaBooks, 2012.

Khalsa, Shanti Shanti Kaur. "The Effects of Two Types of Meditation Techniques on Self-Efficacy Beliefs in Persons in CDC Stages II and III of HIV disease." Ph.D. diss., Columbia Pacific University, 1993.

———. "Supporting People with Posttraumatic Stress Disorder (PTSD) through Kundalini Yoga: Manual for International Kundalini Yoga Therapy Professional Training." Espanola, N.Mex.: Guru Ram Das Center for Medicine & Humanology, 2016.

Kiecolt-Glaser, Janice K., Lisa M. Christian, Rebecca Andridge, Beom Seuk Hwang, William B. Malarkey, Martha A. Belury, Charles F. Emery, and Ronald Glaser. "Adiponectin, Leptin, and Yoga Practice." *Physiology and Behavior* 107, no. 5 (December 2012): 809–13. doi:10.1016/j.physbeh.2012 .01.016.

Krishna, Bandi Hari, Gorantla Shravya Keerthi, Chintala Kiran Kumar, and Natham Mallikarjuna Reddy. "Association of Leukocyte Telomere Length with Oxidative Stress in Yoga Practitioners." *Journal of Clinical and Diagnostic Research* 9, no. 3 (March 2015): CC01–CC03. doi:10.7860 /JCDR/2015/13076.5729.

Lindqvist, Daniel, Elissa S. Epel, Synthia H. Mellon, Brenda W. Penninx, Dóra Révéz, J. E. Verhoeven, Victor I. Reus, et al. "Psychiatric Disorders and Leukocyte Telomere Length: Underlying Mechanisms Linking Mental Illness with Cellular Aging." *Neuroscience and Biobehavioral Reviews* 55 (August 2015): 333–64. doi:10.1016/j.neubiorev.2015.05.007.

Markil, Nina, Michael Whitehurst, Patrick L. Jacobs, and Robert F. Zoeller. "Yoga Nidra Relaxation Increases Heart Rate Variability and Is Unaffected by a Prior Bout of Hatha Yoga." *The Journal of Alternative and Complementary Medicine* 18, no. 10 (October 2012): 953–58. doi:10.1089 /acm.2011.0331.

McEwen, Bruce S. "Protective and Damaging Effects of Stress Mediators." *The New England Journal of Medicine* 338, no. 3 (January 1998): 171–79. doi:10.1056/NEJM199801153380307.

Meyerhoff, Dieter J., Anderson Mon, Thomas Metzler, and Thomas. C. Neylan. "Cortical Gamma-Aminobutyric Acid and Glutamate in Posttraumatic Stress Disorder and Their Relationships to Self-Reported Sleep Quality." *Sleep* 37, no. 5 (May 2014): 893–900. doi:10.5665/sleep.3654.

Minassian, Arpi, Adam X. Maihofer, Dewleen G. Baker, Caroline M. Nievergelt, Mark A. Geyer, and Victoria B. Risbrough. "Association of Predeployment Heart Rate Variability with Risk of Postdeployment Posttraumatic Stress Disorder in Active-Duty Marines." *JAMA Psychiatry* 72, no. 10 (October 2015): 979–86. doi:10.1001/jamapsychiatry.2015.0922.

Mitchell, Matthew D., Philip Gehrman, Michael Perlis, and Craig A. Umscheid. "Comparative Effectiveness of Cognitive Behavioral Therapy for Insomnia: A Systematic Review." *BMC Family Practice* 13 (May 2012): 40. doi:10.1186/1471-2296-13-40.

Mitchell, Stephen, trans., *Tao Te Ching*. New York City: Harper Perennial, 1988.

Moreira, Fernanda Pedrotti, Tiane de Azevedo Cardoso, Thaíse Campos Mondin, Luciano Dias de Mattos Souza, Ricardo Silva, Karen Jansen, Jean Pierre Oses, and Carolina David Wiener. "The Effect of Proinflammatory Cytokines in Cognitive Behavioral Therapy." *Journal of Neuroimmunology* 285 (August 2015): 143–46. doi:10.1016/j.jneuroim.2015.06.004.

Nishith, Pallavi, Stephen P. Duntley, Peter P. Domitrovich, Matthew L. Uhles, Brenda J. Cook, and Phyllis K. Stein. "Effect of Cognitive Behavioral Therapy on Heart Rate Variability during REM Sleep in Female Rape Victims With PTSD." *Journal of Traumatic Stress* 16, no. 3 (June 2003): 247–50. doi:10.1023/a:1023791906879.

O'Doherty, D. C., K. M. Chitty, S. Saddiqui, M. R. Bennett, and J. Lagopoulos. "A Systematic Review and Meta-Analysis of Magnetic Resonance Imaging Measurement of Structural Volumes in Posttraumatic Stress Disorder." *Psychiatry Research* 232, no. 1 (April 2015): 1–33.

Pascoe, Michaela C., and Isabelle E. Bauer. "A Systematic Review of Randomized Control Trials on the Effects of Yoga on Stress Measures and Mood." *Journal of Psychiatric Research* 68 (September 2015): 270–82. doi:10.1016/j.jpsychires.2015.07.013.

Passos, Ives C., Mirela Paiva Vasconcelos-Moreno, Leonardo Gazzi Costa, Maurício Kunz, Elisa Brietzke, João Quevedo, Giovanni Salum, et al. "Inflammatory Markers in Post-Traumatic Stress Disorder: A Systematic Review, Meta-Analysis, and Meta-Regression." *Lancet Psychiatry* 2, no. 11 (November 2015): 1002–12. doi:10.1016/S2215-0366(15)00309-0.

Pissiota, Anna, Örjan Frans, Manuel Fernandez, Lars von Knorring, Håkan Fischer, and Mats Fredrikson. "Neurofunctional Correlates of Posttraumatic Stress Disorder: A PET Symptom Provocation Study." *European Archives of Psychiatry and Clinical Neuroscience* 252, no. 2 (April 2002): 68–75. doi:10.1007/s004060200014.

Prabhavananda, Swami, and Christopher Isherwood "Yoga and Its Aims." Chap. 1 in *How to Know God: The Yoga Aphorisms of Patanjali.* Hollywood, Calif.: The Vedanta Society of Southern California, 1981.

Quiñones, Natalia, Yvonne Gómez Maquet, Diana María Agudelo Vélez, and Maria Adeliada López. "Efficacy of a Satyananda Yoga Intervention for Reintegrating Adults Diagnosed with Posttraumatic Stress Disorder." *International Journal of Yoga Therapy* 25, no. 1 (2015): 89–99. doi:10.17761/1531-2054-25.1.89.

Rajbhoj, Pratibha H., Sanjay Uddhav Shete, Anita Verma, and Ranjit Singh Bhogal. "Effect of Yoga Module on Pro-Inflammatory and Anti-Inflammatory Cytokines in Industrial Workers of Lonavla: A Randomized Controlled Trial." *Journal of Clinical and Diagnostic Research* 9, no. 2 (February 2015): CC01–CC05. doi:10.7860/JCDR/2015/11426.5551.

Rhodes, Alison, Joseph Spinazzola, and Bessel van der Kolk. "Yoga for Adult Women With Chronic PTSD: A Long-Term Follow-up Study." *The Journal of Alternative and Complementary Medicine* 22, no. 3 (March 2016): 189–96. doi:10.1089/acm.2014.0407.

Ross, Alyson, Erika Friedmann, Margaret Bevans, and Sue Thomas. "Frequency of Yoga Practice Predicts Health: Results of a National Survey of Yoga Practitioners." *Evidence-Based Complementary and Alternative Medicine* 2012 (2012): 983258. doi:10.1155/2012/983258.

Santaella, Danilo F., Cesar R. S. Devesa, Marcos R. Rojo, Marcelo B. P. Amato, Lucian F. Drager, Karina R. Casali, Nicola Montano, and Geraldo Lorenzi-Filho. "Yoga Respiratory Training Improves Respiratory Function and Cardiac Sympathovagal Balance in Elderly Subjects: A Randomized Controlled Trial." *BMJ Open* 1, no. 1 (May 2011): e000085. doi:10.1136/bmjopen-2011-000085.

Seppälä, Emma M., Jack B. Nitschke, Dana L. Tudorascu, Andrea Hayes, Micheal R. Goldstein, Dong T. H. Nguyen, David Perlman, and Richard J. Davidson. "Breathing-Based Meditation Decreases Posttraumatic Stress Disorder Symptoms in U.S. Military Veterans: A Randomized Controlled Longitudinal Study." *Journal of Traumatic Stress* 27, no. 4 (August 2014): 397–405. doi:10.1002/jts.21936.

Shin, Lisa M., Scott L. Rauch, and Roger K. Pitman. "Amygdala, Medial Prefrontal Cortex, and Hippocampal Function in PTSD." *Annals of the New York Academy of Sciences* 1071 (July 2006): 67–79. doi:10.1196 /annals.1364.007.

Shin, Lisa M., Paul J. Whalen, Roger K. Pitman, George Bush, Michael L. Macklin, Natasha B. Lasko, Scott P. Orr, Sean C. McInerney, and Scott L. Rauch. "An FMRI Study of Anterior Cingulate Function in Posttraumatic Stress Disorder." *Biological Psychiatry* 50, no. 12 (December 2001): 932–42. doi:10.1016/s0006-3223(01)01215-x.

Sovik, Rolf, and Ananda Balayogi Bhavanani. "History, Philosophy, and Practice of Yoga." Chap. 2 in *The Principles and Practice of Yoga in Healthcare,* edited by Sat Bir Singh Khalsa, Lorenzo Cohen, Timothy McCall, and Shirley Telles. Pencaitland, Scottland: Handspring Publishing Limited, 2016.

Spicuzza, Lucia, Alessandra Gabutti, Cesare Porta, Nicola Montano, and Luciano Bernardi. "Yoga and Chemoreflex Response to Hypoxia and Hypercapnia." *Lancet* 356, no. 9240 (October 2000): 1495–96. doi:10.1016 /s0140-6736(00)02881-6.

Staples, Julie K., Michelle F. Hamilton, and Madeline Uddo. "A Yoga Program for the Symptoms of Post-Traumatic Stress Disorder in Veterans." *Military Medicine* 178, no. 8 (August 2013): 854–60. doi:10.7205 /MILMED-D-12-00536.

Staples, Julie K., Daniel Mintie, and Sat Bir Singh Khalsa. "Evaluation of a Combined Yoga and Cognitive Behavioral Therapy Program for Posttraumatic Stress Disorder." *Journal of Alternative and Complementary Medicine* 22, no. 6 (2016): A94. doi:10.1089/acm.2016.29003.abstracts.

Strecher, Victor J., Brenda McEvoy DeVellis, Marshall H. Becker, and Irwin M. Rosenstock. "The Role of Self-Efficacy in Achieving Health Behavior Change." *Health Education Quarterly* 13, no. 1 (1986): 73–92. doi:10.1177/109019818601300108.

Streeter, Chris C., J. Eric Jensen, Ruth M. Perlmutter, Howard J. Cabral, Hua

Tian, Devin B. Terhune, Domenic A. Ciraulo, and Perry F. Renshaw. "Yoga Asana Sessions Increase Brain GABA Levels: A Pilot Study." *The Journal of Alternative and Complementary Medicine* 13, no. 4 (May 2007): 419–26. doi:10.1089/acm.2007.6338.

Streeter, Chris C., Theodore H. Whitfield, Liz Owen, Tasha Rein, Surya K. Karri, Aleksandra Yakhkind, Ruth Perlmutter, et al. "Effects of Yoga versus Walking on Mood, Anxiety, and Brain GABA Levels: A Randomized Controlled MRS Study." *The Journal of Alternative and Complementary Medicine* 16, no. 11 (August 2010): 1145–52. doi:10.1089/acm.2010.0007.

Szabó, Csilla, Oguz Kelemen, and Szabolcs Kéri. "Changes in FKBP5 Expression and Memory Functions during Cognitive-Behavioral Therapy in Posttraumatic Stress Disorder: A Preliminary Study." *Neuroscience Letters* 569 (May 2014): 116–20. doi: 10.1016/j.neulet.2014.03.059.

Telles, Shirley, R. Nagarathna, and H. R. Nagendra. "Breathing through a Particular Nostril Can Alter Metabolism and Autonomic Activities." *Indian Journal of Physiology and Pharmacology* 38, no. 2 (April 1994): 133–37.

Trousselard, Marion, Bertrand Lefebvre, Lionel Caillet, Yann Andruetan, Franck de Montleau, Josaine Denis, and Frédéric Canini. "Is Plasma GABA Level a Biomarker of Post-Traumatic Stress Disorder (PTSD) Severity? A Preliminary Study." *Psychiatry Research* 241 (July 2016): 273–79. doi: 10.1016/j.psychres.2016.05.013.

van der Kolk, Bessel A., Laura Stone, Jennifer West, Alison Rhodes, David Emerson, Michael Suvak, and Joseph Spinazzola. "Yoga as an Adjunctive Treatment for Posttraumatic Stress Disorder: A Randomized Controlled Trial." *The Journal of Clinical Psychiatry* 75, no. 6 (June 2014): e559–e565. doi:10.4088/jcp.13m08561.

Villemure, Chantal, Marta Čeko, Valerie A. Cotton, and M. Catherine Bushnell. "Neuroprotective Effects of Yoga Practice: Age-, Experience-, and Frequency-Dependent Plasticity." *Frontiers in Human Neuroscience* 9 (May 2015): 281. doi:10.3389/fnhum.2015.00281.

Wang, Zhewu, and M. Rita I. Young. "PTSD, a Disorder with an Immunological Component." *Frontiers in Immunology* 7 (June 2016): 219. doi:10.3389/fimmu.2016.00219.

Wittgenstein, Ludwig. *On Certainty*, edited by G. E. M. Anscombe, and

G. H. von Wright., translated by Denis Paul, and G. E. M. Anscombe. Malden, Mass.: Blackwell Publishing, 1969.

Xie, Lulu, Hongyi Kang, Qiwu Xu, Michael J. Chen, Yonghong Liao, Meenakshisundaram Thiyagarajan, John Donnell, et al. "Sleep Drives Metabolite Clearance from the Adult Brain." *Science* 342, no. 6156 (October 2013): 373–77. doi:10.1126/science.1241224.

Index

Page numbers in *italics* indicate illustrations.

About the Authors

Photo by Daniel Forest

Daniel Mintie, LCSW, is a cognitive-behavioral therapist and researcher who has been healing trauma since 1990. He has a private clinical practice in Taos, New Mexico, and is available via the internet for off-site therapy and professional consultation worldwide. Daniel teaches the cognitive-behavioral therapy portion of the Integrative Trauma Recovery Program. His website is **www.danielmintie.com**.

Photo by Matt Blasing Photography

Julie K. Staples, Ph.D., received a doctorate in Cell and Molecular Biology at St. Louis University. She is the research director at the Center for Mind-Body Medicine in Washington, D.C., and an adjunct assistant professor at Georgetown University School of Medicine. She has been a certified Kundalini Yoga teacher since 1996. Julie teaches online courses on the basics of research and the science of yoga to health care practitioners, yoga teachers, and yoga therapists. She also teaches the yoga portion of the Integrative Trauma Recovery Program. Her website is **www.awarenesstechnologies.net**.

BOOKS OF RELATED INTEREST

Overcoming Acute and Chronic Pain
Keys to Treatment Based on Your Emotional Type
by Marc S. Micozzi, M.D., Ph.D., and Sebhia Marie Dibra

Emotion and Healing in the Energy Body
A Handbook of Subtle Energies in Massage and Yoga
by Robert Henderson

Adaptogens
Herbs for Strength, Stamina, and Stress Relief
by David Winston and Steven Maimes

The Healing Intelligence of Essential Oils
The Science of Advanced Aromatherapy
by Kurt Schnaubelt, Ph.D.

Total Life Cleanse
A 28-Day Program to Detoxify and Nourish the
Body, Mind, and Soul
by Jonathan Glass, M.Ac., C.A.T.

Yoga for Cancer
A Guide to Managing Side Effects, Boosting Immunity,
and Improving Recovery for Cancer Survivors
by Tari Prinster
Foreword by Cyndi Lee

Ayurveda: A Life of Balance
The Complete Guide to Ayurvedic Nutrition and
Body Types with Recipes
by Maya Tiwari

Indigenous Healing Psychology
Honoring the Wisdom of the First Peoples
by Richard Katz, Ph.D.

INNER TRADITIONS • BEAR & COMPANY
P.O. Box 388 • Rochester, VT 05767
1-800-246-8648 • www.InnerTraditions.com

Or contact your local bookseller